Robert A. Goehlich

Make-or-Buy Decisions in Aerospace Organizations

GABLER EDITION WISSENSCHAFT

Robert A. Goehlich

Make-or-Buy Decisions in Aerospace Organizations

Essays on Strategic Efficiency Improvements

With a foreword by
Prof. Dominique Demougin, Ph.D.

GABLER EDITION WISSENSCHAFT

Bibliographic information published by the Deutsche Nationalbibliothek
The Deutsche Nationalbibliothek lists this publication in the Deutsche Nationalbibliografie;
detailed bibliographic data are available in the Internet at http://dnb.d-nb.de.

Dissertation European Business School, International University
Schloss Reichartshausen, Oestrich-Winkel, 2008

D 1540

1st Edition 2009

All rights reserved
© Gabler | GWV Fachverlage GmbH, Wiesbaden 2009

Editorial Office: Claudia Jeske / Britta Göhrisch-Radmacher

Gabler is part of the specialist publishing group Springer Science+Business Media.
www.gabler.de

No part of this publication may be reproduced, stored in a retrieval system or transmitted, in any form or by any means, electronic, mechanical, photocopying, recording, or otherwise, without the prior written permission of the copyright holder.

Registered and/or industrial names, trade names, trade descriptions etc. cited in this publication are part of the law for trade-mark protection and may not be used free in any form or by any means even if this is not specifically marked.

Cover design: Regine Zimmer, Dipl.-Designerin, Frankfurt/Main
Printed on acid-free paper

ISBN 978-3-8349-1530-6

Foreword

Robert A. Goehlich's doctoral thesis analyzes the inefficiencies in today's organizations and the potential explanations for them. According to the thesis, these inefficiencies may be rooted in corporate governance, at least partly as a result of political considerations, as well as for reasons related to the individuals involved and to globalization. Specifically, the thesis focuses on the make-or-buy decision within aerospace organizations.

The second chapter offers an extensive overview of the current aerospace sector from an economic point of view. The chapter has benefited from the background of the author, who has an extensive work experience with JAXA, NASA and EADS.

The third chapter presents the outsourcing strategies that have been employed by space organizations in Europe, the US and Japan. The chapter includes valuable information with respect to existing theories on the make-or-buy decision and its interaction with respect to the aerospace industry in the "big three" regions of the world. The literature used is well explained and its relationship to decisions of organizations in the specific context analyzed is well described.

The fourth chapter describes a theory-based decision process and suggests a very useful tool for guiding management in its make-or-buy decision process. The tool is designed to induce transparency in a modular fashion. Methodologically, the chapter presents sequentially each of the arguments related to make versus buy: the pros and cons of vertical integration and outsourcing. Each of the tool's dimensions has a thorough theoretical foundation with a solid underpinning in the existing literature. The comprehensive method employed by this tool guarantees that management will be forced to think through each of the possible pros and cons of outsourcing versus integration. Including arguments for or against outsourcing in the tool is simplified because the tool is structured in modules. Although developed for the aerospace industry, use of the tool is by no means restricted to that industry.

Overall, the thesis is well written and provides a very useful management tool for guiding the make-or-buy decision processes in organizations.

Prof. Dominique Demougin, Ph.D.
Head of Department of Law, Governance & Economics
European Business School

Acknowledgements

I would like to thank my doctoral supervisor, Prof. Dominique Demougin of the European Business School, Department of Law, Governance & Economics, for the chance to pursue my doctoral studies under his supervision. His advice and guidance for finding the "path to becoming an economist" over the last years, starting from our first meeting in summer 2004, combined with the freedom to develop creativity in these studies, has been a very stimulating combination to me. My acknowledgement goes to Prof. André Schmidt, field of international economic policy at the European Business School, for his ideas, time and effort as a second advisor. His view of economic policy in our meetings has given me a unique chance to incorporate them within my thesis. I am appreciative to the chairman of my doctoral committee, Prof. Hartmut Kreikebaum, field of business ethics and the members, Prof. Stefan Walter and Prof. Michael Henkel, field of supply chain management at the European Business School for accepting my thesis and the time spent on evaluations.

I wish to thank Prof. Rose Rubin, University of Memphis, for helpful comments to the characteristics chapter. Many thanks go to Dr. Veikko Thiele, University of British Columbia, for reviewing the case study chapter. Prof. Ralf Bebenroth of Kobe University is the co-author of this study. I am very grateful for the opportunity to conduct research on this topic with him and for many fruitful discussions as a good friend. Valuable comments from Prof. Benjamin Bental of the University of Haifa on the make-or-buy decision chapter are highly appreciated.

I would like to express my sincere thanks to my colleagues Dr. Sabine Altiparmak, Gudrun Fehler, Petra Ernst and Clemens Buchen of the European Business School for their valuable comments on my thesis and research colloquium regarding content and language, for being so supportive, and for providing a friendly working climate in the department.

I would also like to thank the participants at the 4th International Conference on Economics and Globalization (EcoTrend) 2007 held in Targu Jiu, the International Conference on Applied Business Research (ICABR) 2008 held in Accra and the 18th International Conference of International Trade & Finance Association (IT&FA) 2008 held in Lisbon for their comments and suggestions.

My thanks to my former colleagues, Prof. Anja Schöttner, Dr. Ria Steiger, Dr. Jenny Kragl and Dorothee Schneider of the 2007 disbanded Walther Rathenau Institute for Organization Theory at Humboldt University at Berlin for the nice working climate and answering every silly question a new economist could have.

Last, and most importantly, I would like to thank my parents, Rosemarie and Lothar Goehlich, without whom I would never have been able to achieve so much and who taught me to stay the course even when it is very challenging. In particular, I want to thank my girlfriend Naoko Ogawa, my parents and my sister Anja Wollenberg, for being so patient; the leisure time we spent together was definitely too little in the last years.

This research has been supported by the Alexander von Humboldt Foundation, which is gratefully acknowledged. The views reported in this thesis are those of me alone, and not those of any institution. All errors and omissions, which may unwittingly remain, are the sole responsibility of me.

Robert A. Goehlich

Abstract

Today's organizations suffer from inefficiencies that may occur for any number of reasons. Inefficiencies may: be rooted in the corporate governance of an organization, result from political reasons, be due to individual reasons, and result from globalization as well.

This study focuses on the strategic aspects of decision-making within aerospace organizations, concentrating on the make-or-buy decision in an attempt to examine organizational efficiencies. The present study includes an understanding of the existing organizational structures of aerospace enterprises, and while searching for efficiencies, discusses strategies to avoid inefficiencies and investigates the potential for implementing recommendations into practice.

The main result of the study is the formation of a process, in the form of a computerized tool, that handles approximately 50 propositions of make-or-buy decisions, systematically connected to strategic objectives, and organizational, product and environmental characteristics. The strength of this process lies in its ability to cover the entire spectrum of make-or-buy (the continuum from in-house to buy-off-the-shelf) in order to support decision-makers with holistic recommendations. This process allows one to determine the kind of organizational architecture that is best suited to a specified activity.

The resulting tool is applied to four case studies taken from the aerospace sector: (A) Copy machine usage (as a reference), (B) Aircraft final assembly production, (C) Satellite rocket launch operation and (D) Space tourism rocket development. In three of the four cases, the make-or-buy decision that is recommended by the tool mirrors instinctual, experience-based conclusions. It is also shown that a well considered make-or-buy decision approach is paramount to overcoming operational inefficiencies for aerospace organizations.

Keywords:	Aerospace Organization, Aviation, Corporate Governance, Game Theory, Make-or-Buy Decision, Outsourcing, Strategy, Space, Vertical Integration
JEL Classification:	L25, D23, L93, C72, M55
Statistics:	136 pages, 23 figures, 15 tables, 182 references
Contact:	E-mail: robert@goehlich.com

Table of Contents

Foreword v

Acknowledgements vii

Abstract ix

Table of Contents xi

List of Figures and Tables xiii

List of Abbreviations xv

Definitions xvii

1   Introduction 1

     1.1   Motivation 1

     1.2   Structure and Analytical Procedure 2

     1.3   The Need for Efficiency, Organizations and Multinational Acting 3

2   Economic Characteristics of Aerospace Organizations 7

     2.1   Introduction 7

     2.2   Characteristics 8

         2.2.1   General 8

         2.2.2   Market Structure 9

         2.2.3   Products 9

         2.2.4   Contractor Classification 10

         2.2.5   Industry Size 11

         2.2.6   Organizational Architecture 13

         2.2.7   Performance 20

     2.3   Discussion 21

     2.4   Results 23

3   Outsourcing Strategies in Europe, USA and Japan: A Case of Space Organizations 25

     3.1   Introduction 25

     3.2   Theoretical Approaches for Outsourcing 27

         3.2.1   General 27

         3.2.2   Transaction Cost Theory 27

         3.2.3   Principal-Agent Theory 28

         3.2.4   The Human Resource-based View 29

3.3	Case Study of Space Organizations	30
	3.3.1 General	30
	3.3.2 Europe	32
	3.3.3 USA	33
	3.3.4 Japan	34
3.4	Discussion	35
	3.4.1 General	35
	3.4.2 Understanding of Coherences	36
	3.4.3 Alternative Theories	36
	3.4.4 Limitations	37
3.5	Results	37

4 Development of a Make-or-Buy Decision-supporting Process **39**

4.1	Introduction	39
4.2	The Process	41
	4.2.1 General	41
	4.2.2 Qualitative Assessment	45
	4.2.3 Quantitative Assessment	72
4.3	Application of Process	78
	4.3.1 General	78
	4.3.2 Case Studies	79
	4.3.3 Results	80
4.4	Discussion	87
	4.4.1 General	87
	4.4.2 Choice of Items for "Settings" Submodule	87
	4.4.3 Sensitivity Analysis	88
	4.4.4 Informal Versus Formal Statements	89
	4.4.5 Comparison With Other Studies	90
	4.4.6 Limitations	92
4.5	Results	93

5 Conclusion **95**

References **99**

About the Author **117**

List of Figures and Tables

Figure 1: Research Structure 2

Figure 2: Investigated Characteristics of Aerospace Organizations 8

Figure 3: Number of Manufacturing Plants and Associated Revenue for the US
Aerospace Industry (US Department of Commerce, 1995) 12

Figure 4: Direct Labor Requirement and Annual Output for Lockheed L1011
Aircraft Production (Benkard, 2000) 16

Figure 5: Vision Versus Reality of Space Shuttle Operation (NASA, 2000b) 18

Figure 6: Illustration of Organizational Architectures 39

Figure 7: Overview of the Make-or-Buy Decision-supporting Process 42

Figure 8: Settings Submodule 42

Figure 9: Integration Pros Submodule 43

Figure 10: Outsourcing Pros Submodule 44

Figure 11: Results Submodule 45

Figure 12: Example of a Vertical Integration Proposition 45

Figure 13: Potential-probability Matrix for Vertical Integration 73

Figure 14: Potential-probability Matrix for Outsourcing 75

Figure 15: Integration and Outsourcing Sub-benefit for Each Setting Item (Res01
Output Mask) 78

Figure 16: Application of the Make-or-Buy Decision-supporting Process 80

Figure 17: Extract from the MoB-Tool 81

Figure 18: Sub-benefit for Case Study "(A) Copy Machine" (Res02 Output Mask) 84

Figure 19: Sub-benefit for Case Study "(B) Aircraft" (Res02 Output Mask) 84

Figure 20: Sub-benefit for Case Study "(C) Satellite" (Res02 Output Mask) 85

Figure 21: Sub-benefit for Case Study "(D) Space Tourism" (Res02 Output Mask) ... 85

Figure 22: Outsourcing/Integration Total Benefit Ratio (Res03 Output Mask) 86

Figure 23: Result of Sensitivity Analysis 89

Table 1:	Typical Aviation Market Structure (marked in gray)	9
Table 2:	Typical Space Market Structure (marked in gray)	9
Table 3:	Primary Aerospace Products	10
Table 4:	Classification of Aerospace Contractors	11
Table 5:	Plant Size Distribution of US Aviation Industry (modified from: US Department of Commerce, 1995)	13
Table 6:	Plant Size Distribution of US Space Industry (modified from: US Department of Commerce, 1995)	13
Table 7:	Aerospace Companies Ranked by Revenue (based on: Anselmo, 2005)	20
Table 8:	Comparison of Space Market Structures for Commercial Launchers	31
Table 9:	Vertical Integration Propositions	73
Table 10:	Outsourcing Propositions	74
Table 11:	Integration Pros Submodule	76
Table 12:	Outsourcing Pros Submodule	77
Table 13:	Settings Submodule (Input Mask 1/3)	82
Table 14:	Settings Submodule (Input Mask 2/3)	82
Table 15:	Settings Submodule (Input Mask 3/3)	83

List of Abbreviations

ave.	average
B$	billion US dollars
BERI	Business Environment Risk Index
BLS	Boeing Launch Services
CCC	China Compulsory Certification
CEO	Chief Executive Officer
CNES	Centre National d'Etudes Spatiales
CSA	Chinese Space Agency
EADS	European Aeronautic Defense and Space Company
ESA	European Space Agency
EU	European Union
FFP	Firm-Fixed Price contract
FPIS	Fixed-Price Incentive Successive targets contract
GECAS	General Electric Commercial Aviation Services
GDP	Gross Domestic Product
GPS	Global Positioning System
GTO	Geostationary Transfer Orbit
IHI	Ishikawajima Heavy Industries
ILFC	International Lease Finance Corporation
IR&D	Investor Relations & Development
ISAS	Institute of Space and Astronautical Science
ISO	International Organization for Standardization
ISRO	Indian Space Research Organization
ISS	International Space Station
JAXA	Japan Aerospace Exploration Agency
KPI	Key Performance Indicator
LEO	Low Earth Orbit
LSE	Large Scale Enterprise
M$	million US dollars
MHI	Mitsubishi Heavy Industries
n	number of units built

no.	number
NAL	National Aerospace Laboratory of Japan
NASA	National Aeronautics and Space Administration
NASDA	National Space Development Agency of Japan
NPV	Net Present Value
p	learning rate
R&D	Research and Development
RLV	Reusable Launch Vehicle
RSA	Russian Space Agency
SRB	Solid Rocket Booster
SSME	Space Shuttle Main Engine
w/o	without

Definitions

The following definitions may be useful for understanding the technical terms used in the present study. All numbers, physical units and dates refer to metric systems and are in European style unless otherwise specified. The fiscal year of dollar values is the year of the reference's publication unless otherwise specified.

Expendable Launch Vehicle	A vehicle that can only be used once, that is expended (burnt up) after a single use. All conventional rockets fall under this category.
Reusable Launch Vehicle	A vehicle that can be used multiple times. Note that the Space Shuttle is not a true Reusable Launch Vehicle (RLV) because it requires a new fuel tank for each launch.
Orbital Space Flight	The spacecraft is able to reach and maintain Low Earth Orbit (LEO), which is normally at an altitude of about 200 km.
Space Tourism	Space tourism is the term broadly applied to the concept of paying customers traveling beyond Earth's atmosphere.
Suborbital Space Flight	The spacecraft is able to reach astronaut altitude, but is not traveling at a speed fast enough to maintain an Earth orbit. The total flight will last about ½ hour or maximal 3 hours if using a carrier aircraft depending on the type of vehicle and flight profile used.

1 Introduction

This chapter aims to provide an overview of the motivation, structure and analytical procedure of the present research series. Further, the chapter briefly introduces the need for efficiency, the need for building organizations as well as the need for thinking and acting on a multinational level. These are pivotal topics found in all three studies of the present research series.

1.1 Motivation

The primary purpose of this research series is to find strategies that promise to increase the efficiencies of aerospace organizations. Research in the field of "efficiency of organizations" is immense, but mostly disregards inefficiencies that occur uniquely for aerospace organizations. Economic literature typically addresses the make-or-buy decision with regard to only a few industry sectors (e.g., coal, oil, gas, electric, agriculture, IT business, automobile, trucking), but seldom broaches the aerospace sector and does not yet address the space sector as a central topic.

However, aerospace organizations offer much potential for efficiency improvements (see US Congress, 1995; A.T. Kearney, 2003). Their importance to global market output strongly increases over the last several decades and this trend is expected to continue in the future. Thus, this research series aims to offer some insights into this relatively unexplored arena.

Among others, the make-or-buy decision is a trade-off between the diseconomies of scope (make) and the transaction costs that are caused by search frictions, incomplete contracts and relation-specific investments (buy). Current theories indicate why, when stressing efficiency gains in terms of transaction and production costs, certain activities might best be suited for outsourcing; while other theories show that particular activities, e.g., core competencies, are more efficient when vertically integrated.

However, real-world outsourcing decisions are seldom based on the sound trade-off of risk, on the costs imposed and the potential benefits of these risks. One reason for this is the overwhelming supply of theories, each one concentrating on a single aspect of the problem and therefore complicating the decision-making process for managers. Thus, there is a need for a process that: (1) is simple to apply; (2) encompasses the various predictions that are typically tested in isolation in the empirical literature; and (3) allows significant conclusions to be drawn that are aligned with extant theories related to the make-or-buy decision.

The present investigation also attempts to overcome literature shortcomings by developing a process through which trade-off is made essential to analysis. Partnerships have both positive and negative effects. By explaining these effects, the present study attempts to enhance the current understanding of both efficient vertical integration and outsourcing.

1.2 Structure and Analytical Procedure

This research series is structured in three studies, starting with one overview study (Chapter 2) followed by two in-depth studies (Chapter 3 and 4), as illustrated in Figure 1. Each investigated issue and the related results are presented as a separate chapter, however, the investigation is performed in conjunction with all three studies. The chapters titled "Introduction" and "Conclusion" are not represented in this figure.

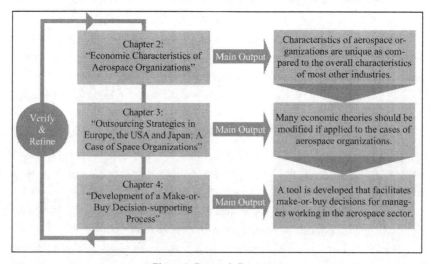

Figure 1: Research Structure

Chapter 2, titled "Economic Characteristics of Aerospace Organizations," provides an overview and discussion of the typical characteristics of aerospace organizations from an economic perspective. Chapter 3, titled "Outsourcing Strategies in Europe, the

USA and Japan: A Case of Space Organizations," examines the applicability of organizational theories to space organizations' outsourcing activities. Chapter 4, titled "Development of a Make-or-Buy Decision-supporting Process," investigates the make-or-buy decision in detail and offers a tool to incorporate all theoretically known advantages and disadvantages of vertical integration or outsourcing, respectively.

For all three studies, the investigated system architecture within this research series is defined using system elements, geopolitical structures and time frames:

- **System Elements:** In the present study, the term "aerospace organization" means companies that operate in the aerospace industry, as well as aerospace agencies and any other unions or alliances that concern aerospace. The term "aerospace" includes: aircraft, aircraft engines, space vehicles, space vehicle propulsion units, missiles and space systems.

- **Geopolitical Structures:** The USA, Europe, Japan, Russia, China and India mainly contribute to the space sector, while the USA and Europe not only contribute to the space sector, but also contribute primarily to the aviation sector. Therefore, this study focuses on these six regions. All six regions are stable in terms of economic and political issues within the investigated time frame.

- **Time Frames:** The time frame of the investigated case studies and scenarios is 1980-2026.

1.3 The Need for Efficiency, Organizations and Multinational Acting

Here, I briefly introduce the need for efficiency, the need for building organizations as well as the need for thinking and acting on a multinational level. These pivotal topics are found in all three studies of the present research series.

- **The Need for Efficiency:** Due to high demand for the long-term reliability of aircraft systems, the aviation sector is cost-intensive. Substantial demand for reliability exists because a high catastrophic failure rate does not meet ethical standards and is too costly. In a similar way, this phenomenon can be applied to the space sector as well. Government funding was often approved only in the hope for political gains or for national security reasons. As a result, space organizations have relied on government subsidies, allowing them to become notoriously inefficient in their use of working capital (A.T. Kearney, 2003).

In order to improve safety and reduce costs in the long term, greater overall efficiency is constantly required in the industry.

- **The Need for Building Organizations:** Because of increasing labor returns, a team of workers can produce more output than the same number of single workers. This creates an incentive for workers to build a team, which in turn, results in the formation of organizations (Arrow, 1970; Tirole, 1988). Potential sources of improving labor returns primarily include the division of labor within each group of the organization that concentrates on a particular task. Related to this is the possibility of specialization, with the effect of learning-by-doing when experience improves workers' skills.

  However, a team's output may marginally diminish from a certain point when more workers are added to the team. First, efficiency decreases when one worker's tasks interfere with those of a colleague. Second, monitoring costs increase when another job or worker is necessary in order to manage and monitor worker performances. In addition, monitoring creates also a moral hazard problem because monitoring precision is not verifiable (Bental & Demougin, 2006). Thus, according to Coase (1937), an organization should expand only so long as the costs of an additional transaction within the organization do not surpass market costs. Gibbons (2005) provides an overall integrative framework of the various elemental theories of organizations as put forth by Grossman, Hart, Holmstrom, Klein, Moore, Murphy, Simon, Williamson, etc.

- **The Need for Thinking and Acting on a Multinational Level:** In particular, the very high costs of aerospace programs (e.g., the Space Shuttle's Main Engine (SSME) development costs are $6,3 billion (Koelle, 2003), the Airbus A380's development costs are $12 billion (Phillips, 2005) and the International Space Station's (ISS) operational costs are $5,5 billion per year (David, 2002)) necessitate the formation and/or cooperation of both national and multinational aerospace organizations.

  Worldwide, aerospace organizations adopt an approach of simultaneous cooperation and competition. For example, the USA cooperates with Russia, Europe and Japan in endeavors that concern the International Space Station (ISS), but the USA competes with these countries with regard to its commercial satellites. A dilemma, therefore, exists because Organization A (e.g., a national enterprise), may desire a collaborative relationship with Organization B (e.g., a foreign enterprise) that enhances productivity and growth. However, due to national security interests, Organization A does not want Organization B to acquire sensitive technology that could be used for military purposes one day or, does not want to support Organization B competition's efforts.

What kinds of interactions exist between the global aerospace players that are residents of the USA, Europe, Japan, Russia, China and India? Is this "game" driven by fairness, competition and/or cooperation? Game theory facilitates efficient decision-making given this situation.

2 Economic Characteristics of Aerospace Organizations

This chapter provides an overview of the current aerospace sector from an economic point of view, along with possible projections. An aerospace organization shows many different characteristics. These characteristics are selected, which form the basis for the development of follow-up studies within the present research series. The current chapter discusses products manufactured in this industry and the market environment, industry and organizational architecture that exist amidst economic trends.

2.1 Introduction

The aerospace industry has continued to develop since the first motorized flight of the Wright Brothers in 1903. Today, the importance of aerospace to the world's economy is immense.

One option used to measure the importance of aeronautics to the world's economy is by its contribution to Gross Domestic Product (GDP). For example, direct contributions, such as air transportation and indirect contributions, such as aircraft manufacturing or tourism, by the US aviation industry to the US GDP has been estimated at $436 billion per year, or 5% of the US GDP (Anderson, 1999). Another way to consider the importance of aeronautics is the increase in passenger traffic and related aircraft demand. World passenger traffic is expected to increase by around 5% per year according to Airbus' (2008) Global Market Forecast for 2007-2026. Boeing predicts that the total market potential for new commercial airplanes in the course of the next twenty years will be around 29 000 airplanes (Boeing, 2007a). Such market share would require an average annual output of over 1000 planes by the world's commercial aircraft manufacturers alone, which is substantially above the current rate of production (Commission on Engineering and Technical Systems, 1999).

The importance of the space sector to the world's economy is lesser than that of aeronautics, but the space sector plays an important role with regard to improvement in a country's quality of life. For example, operating satellites provide weather and natural catastrophe forecasts, help expose environmental offenders, and facilitate communication, education and telemedicine in remote regions. The space sector is also a critical component of a country's technology base for enhancing and maintaining national security (Lorell & Levaux, 1998).

Thus, the increasing importance and potential of the aerospace sector to the world's economy justifies, encourages and necessitates an economic-based investigation of aerospace organizations, such that it is provided in this research series.

2.2 Characteristics

2.2.1 General

Figure 2 lists the characteristics of organizations that operate in the aviation and/or space sector, which are investigated in this section. Each characteristic could alone be the subject of a lengthy volume of investigation. However, in order to produce a manageable document, the present study focuses on providing summary information for each characteristic. An exception to these summaries is the larger description of organizational architecture found in this study, which is presented due to its valuable information and complexity. Due to national security concerns that are the nature of aerospace, detailed data availability is very limited. Therefore, the characteristics presented in this section are often based on examples from which I have drawn conclusions and/or insights. This overview of the economic characteristics of aerospace organizations provides only a brief, but not complete introduction to the topic. I selected those characteristics that are most promising to deliver important facts for an effective investigation of the make-or-buy decisions that occur in the case of aerospace organizations.

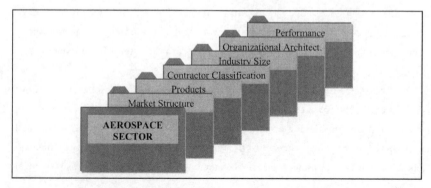

Figure 2: Investigated Characteristics of Aerospace Organizations

Economic Characteristics of Aerospace Organizations 9

2.2.2 Market Structure

Market demand in the aviation and the space sector is disparate. There is demand for the take-off of an aircraft about every second somewhere in the world, while only approximately one rocket is launched every third day worldwide. Typical market structures, formed by market demand, are shown in gray for the aviation sector in Table 1 and for the space sector in Table 2. Examples are given in parenthesis for each case. Examples in white boxes are only for orientation and do not apply to aerospace. As shown in the tables, market power increases from left to right and from top to bottom. Market power is inversely related to the number of organizations, but is stronger for those organizations that produce differentiated products. In summary, competition among many organizations dominates the aviation market, while the space market is driven by only a few powerful organizations.

Table 1: Typical Aviation Market Structure (marked in gray)

Product	Number of Organizations		
	Many	Several	One
Homogeneous	Perfect Competition (e.g., wheat farmers)	Homogeneous Oligopoly (kerosene producers)	Monopoly (e.g., local telephone service)
Differentiated	Monopolistic Competition (airlines)	Differentiated Oligopoly (Airbus and Boeing)	

Table 2: Typical Space Market Structure (marked in gray)

Product	Number of Organizations		
	Many	Several	One
Homogeneous	Perfect Competition (e.g., wheat farmers)	Homogeneous Oligopoly (rocket propellant producers)	Monopoly (ISS modules can only be transported by Space Shuttle)
Differentiated	Monopolistic Competition (e.g., restaurants)	Differentiated Oligopoly (launch service operators)	

2.2.3 Products

This section provides an overview of aerospace products, divided into aviation and space related ones, as shown in Table 3. Examples are given in parenthesis for each case.

There are many different types of aircraft included in this industry, such as airplanes, helicopters, balloons, etc. However, the present study focuses primarily on the production of airplanes since they represent the largest revenue portion of the industry. Major customers of the aircraft industry include commercial airlines, transport companies and the military.

Facilities that produce jet engines and auxiliary parts employ processes that are similar to many other metal casting, fabricating and finishing facilities and processes from a wide range of other industries. Typical products manufactured by these facilities include: engines, exhaust systems, motors, brakes, landing gear, wing assemblies, propellers, etc. The main customers for these industries are the enterprises involved in the assembly of aircraft.

The space vehicle and missile industry includes enterprises that are primarily engaged in the research and manufacturing of the following typical products: guided and ballistic missiles, space and military rockets, space vehicles, propulsion units, engines and airframe assemblies. The main customer for this industry is the military; however, space vehicles are also used by commercial entities for releasing communication satellites.

Table 3: Primary Aerospace Products

Aviation Sector	Space Sector
• Aircraft w/o Engines (Airbus A380, Boeing B 787, Concorde, etc.)	• Space Vehicles w/o Engines (Ariane 5, Space Shuttle, H2-A rocket, etc.)
	• Missiles (Patriot, drones, SS9, etc.)
	• Space Systems (International Space Station, Galileo GPS satellites, Meteosat weather satellite, etc.)
• Jet Engines (Rolls-Royce Trent 900, CFM-56, V2500, etc.)	• Propulsion Units (Space Shuttle Main Engine SSME, Vulcain 2, Solid Rocket Booster SRB, etc.)
• Auxiliary Parts (landing gear, brakes, on-board entertainment system, etc.)	• Auxiliary Parts (landing parachutes, navigation computers, cameras, etc.)
• Infrastructure (Frankfurt airport, SkyChefs catering, Lufthansa Technik maintenance, etc.)	• Infrastructure (Kourou spaceport, Santa Maria ground station, Colibri transport ship, etc.)

2.2.4 Contractor Classification

Manufacturing and assembly of complete units in the aerospace industry typically involves a prime contractor and several tiers of subcontractors as shown in Table 4 (modified from: US Environmental Protection Agency, 1998). The prime contractor sells

Economic Characteristics of Aerospace Organizations 11

complete units to customers, while subcontractors sell to the prime contractor or other subcontractors (US Congress, 1995). The example given in the table is taken from the aviation industry for large aircraft.

While there has not been any foreign content for key aircraft components for early models, such as the Boeing 727 (US companies have produced nose fuselage, front fuselage, center wing box, aft fuselage, wing and empennage), foreign partners have clearly become important for production of current models, such as the Boeing 787 (US companies only produce parts of the nose fuselage, front fuselage and empennage). Also, prime contractors for the B787 model control the selection process of subcontractors, in the same manner as has been done for early models by Boeing (MacPherson & Pritchard, 2007).

Table 4: Classification of Aerospace Contractors

Agents	Tasks	Example
Prime Contractor	Design, develop, assemble and/or manufacture complete units and sell to the customer	Aircraft final assembly and selling to the airline (aircraft)
First-tier Subcontractors	Provide major assembly and/or manufacture of sections of air/spacecraft without design or assembly of complete units	Wing assembly (aircraft parts)
Second-tier Subcontractors	Make various subassemblies and sections	Fuel pump for wing (aircraft parts)
Third-tier Subcontractors	Produce machined components and subassemblies	Electric control unit of fuel pump (variety of industries)
Fourth-tier Subcontractors	Specialize in the production of particular components and processes	Electronic components of electric control unit (variety of industries)
Fifth-tier Subcontractors	Produce basic commodities and/or raw materials	Ceramic for electronic components (variety of industries)

2.2.5 Industry Size

Figure 3 illustrates the distribution of manufacturing plants and the associated revenues within the US aerospace industry. I choose the US aerospace industry as an example because the USA has the largest share, e.g., 55% in 1998 (National Science Board, 2002), of the world's aerospace market, with revenues of $161 billion in 2004 (Euromonitor International, 2005). These figures show that while the "aircraft parts" sector of the US aerospace industry is by far the largest in terms of number of manufacturing plants (59%), the "aircraft" sector generates the most revenue (48%). Revenue produced in 2004 was nearly identical for the military sector and the civil sector (Euromonitor International, 2005). In this study, a manufacturing plant is defined as a single physical location where industrial operations are performed. Thus, a company may have one or many manufacturing plants.

Figure 3 indicates that the aircraft-related portion of the US aerospace industry is much larger than the US space vehicle and missile portion. The aircraft portion comprises approximately 90% of the manufacturing plants and about 80% of the revenues for the industry overall. However, considering the small percentage of plants that are engaged in guided missile and space vehicle manufacturing (2%), revenue is relatively high (15%) for this segment of the industry. In general, there are few plants that are responsible for assembling final aerospace products and their production rates are low, but the value of each of their products greatly surpasses that of the supporting industries.

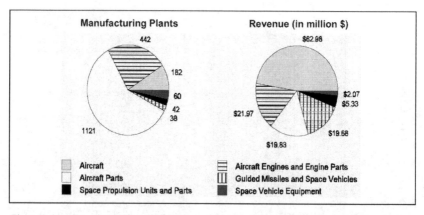

Figure 3: Number of Manufacturing Plants and Associated Revenue for the US Aerospace Industry (US Department of Commerce, 1995)

Table 5 lists the plant size distribution of the aviation sector, while Table 6 lists the plant size distribution of the space sector. The number of aviation plants is strongly decreasing, while there are an increasing number of employees per plant. By contrast, the number of space plants is slightly increasing alongside an increasing number of employees per plant. Thus, aircraft, engine and manufacturing of associated parts generally employs fewer people per plant than space vehicle, missile, propulsion and manufacturing of associated parts. This is due to the fact that, for example, a simple glider can be

Economic Characteristics of Aerospace Organizations 13

produced by a local team of five persons using a few inexpensive tools, while a complex rocket can only be produced by thousands of employees in a plant equipped with expensive tools. However, the number of employees in the aircraft industry (about 650 000) still exceeds that of the space vehicle industries (about 150 000). Note that the aviation industry (1745 plants) is more than ten times larger than the space industry (140 plants) in terms of number of plants.

Table 5: Plant Size Distribution of US Aviation Industry (modified from: US Department of Commerce, 1995)

Plant Size	Aircraft Plants		Aircraft Engines Plants		Associated Parts Plants		Total Plants	
[no. of employees]	[no.]	[%]	[no.]	[%]	[no.]	[%]	[no.]	[%]
1-9	60	33	112	26	480	43	652	37
10-49	42	23	130	29	371	33	543	31
50-249	29	16	129	29	182	16	340	19
250-2499	32	18	63	14	78	7	173	10
2500+	19	10	8	2	10	1	37	2
Total	182	100	442	100	1121	100	1745	100

Table 6: Plant Size Distribution of US Space Industry (modified from: US Department of Commerce, 1995)

Plant Size	Space Vehicles Plants		Propulsion Units Plants		Associated Parts Plants		Total Plants	
[no. of employees]	[no.]	[%]	[no.]	[%]	[no.]	[%]	[no.]	[%]
1-9	4	10	6	14	16	27	26	19
10-49	5	13	8	19	14	23	27	19
50-249	5	13	8	19	18	30	31	22
250-2499	12	32	15	36	10	17	37	26
2500+	12	32	5	12	2	3	19	14
Total	38	100	42	100	60	100	140	100

2.2.6 Organizational Architecture

The aerospace sector, particularly the space sector, is well known for its high quality but also for its costly business as compared to other market sectors. In addition to necessary costs, "Business as Usual" costs in the aerospace sector are caused by excessive specifications, high bureaucracy levels, numerous design changes, extended schedules, parallel work on identical topics, poor and mostly belated communication and too many meetings. Koelle (2003) and Goehlich and Ruecker (2005) list strategies to reduce "Business as Usual" costs in the aerospace sector. Their strategies related to organizational issues are discussed in the following paragraph for the development, production and operational phases of the industry.

a) Development Phase

Success for a buyer (principal) of developing new aerospace systems is strongly related to the type of contract she has with her supplier (agent), the organizational principle of supplier to sub-suppliers and the technique of prototype.

As for the *type of contract*, award fee and fixed price contracts are typically used. Award fee contracts are based on schedule milestones, technical performance and final cost. These contracts provide the contractor with an award when he achieves cost savings. This incentive for the contractor helps to decrease development costs. On the other hand, in a fixed price contract the agent is paid a price for performing a job based on the specifications that are proposed by the principal. Thus, the agent puts in cost-reducing efforts up to the point where the marginal cost of effort equals the marginal benefit. A fixed price contract is more suitable for the production phase, because in the development phase it may cause critical delays in project schedules due to bureaucracy, such as occurs in lengthy negotiations about risk premiums for the agent. Detailed compensation arrangements are investigated by Crocker and Reynolds (1993). In particular in the case of cost uncertainty – typical of the development phase – Jensen and Stonecash (2005) provide a comprehensive overview.

The *organizational principle* for development of a complex program requires a clear-cut prime contractor and subcontractor relationship that includes well-defined responsibilities. Several participating parallel contractors are coordinated by the customer or an additional organization instead of a strong prime contractor, which causes high program costs. For example, reorganization of the responsibility for Space Shuttle operations to only one prime contractor reduced annual costs by 32% compared to the prior practice of awarding five contracts to five different companies working in parallel (Koelle, 2003). Koelle argues that these cost reductions are the result of less manpower, fewer interfaces, fewer planned and unplanned parallel activities, and fewer delays.

As for the *technique of prototype*, the so-called "rapid prototyping" and "step-by-step technique" are commonly used. The aviation industry and private investors favor the rapid prototyping technique. Time-consuming and expensive detailed design and theoretical analyses efforts are replaced by early construction in order to verify the design. A physical likeliness of the product is created directly from a three-dimensional model. The prototypes are accurate in physical dimensions and shape, but do not allow for material properties testing (Slay et al., 1999). An example is the American SR-71 aircraft, which took off only 30 months after the contract had been awarded. The step-by-step technique is favored by the space industry and governments (an exemption is Russian space projects, which successfully realize rapid prototyping). A subscale test vehicle is built if the real-size program cannot be fully funded or technological verification by a full-scale flight vehicle seems indispensable. An example is the Delta Clipper DC-X experimental vehicle developed by McDonnell Douglas or the Phoenix flight test demonstrator developed by EADS Astrium.

b) Production Phase

Different production methods, depending, among other factors, on annual flight or launch rates, respectively, are pursued for economic efficiencies. For a relatively high flight or launch rate, a continuous production activity is maintained, which means scheduled introduction of new vehicles into the program typically occurs in the aviation sector (e.g., daily production of a single aisle aircraft). For a relatively low flight or launch rate, all vehicles plus spares required should be produced in an optimally short time period (in batches) and put into storage until needed, as is typical of the space sector (e.g., batch production of five Space Shuttle orbiters). Production facilities are then converted and used for other projects.

Implementing continuous production in the space sector too, might decrease production costs (including efforts at quality control) tremendously. However, today's market demands do not yet justify producing aerospace systems in high quantity. For example, recent, increasing interest mainly in space tourism, but also in space-based solar power stations, moon or asteroids mining, and very fast delivery services may substantially change current demand-supply interactions (Goehlich, 2005).

In this context, the learning effect on one side and the forgetting effect on the other side are introduced briefly in the next two paragraphs. Despite widely cited examples of learning curves for aircraft production, the marginal costs of producing aircraft represented by direct labor requirements do not always decrease (due to learning effects) and can even increase (due to forgetting effects) slightly over time, as shown in Figure 4.

Benkard (2004) introduces an empirical dynamic oligopoly model of the commercial aircraft industry that is processed in three steps: (1) define a representative model (learning curves, product differentiation, entry costs, strategic interactions, etc.); (2) estimate primitives of the model (state variables for demand and supply, etc.); and (3) run the model (compute equilibrium, compare model results with existing data, evaluate counterfactual policies, determine accuracy, etc.). This model provides a tool to better understand industry pricing, industry performance and optimal industry policy. The novelty of this model is its capability to endogenously determine major characteristics, such as entry, exit, prices and quantities in Markov Perfect Equilibrium. A major result of this model is to explain empirically that a company has an incentive to continually price below static marginal costs instead of exiting the market because of an expectation for future success. Once an airline has decided to buy from Producer A, the airline also has an incentive to buy again from the same producer. That is because airlines prefer fleet commonality – also called the "family concept" – as it reduces operational costs, e.g., the same cockpit layout results in no additional costs for training pilots, the same subsystems result in inexpensive maintenance, etc. Therefore, the producer has also a strong incentive to offer a complete family concept to the airlines; even if one aircraft type's marginal cost is higher than its price.

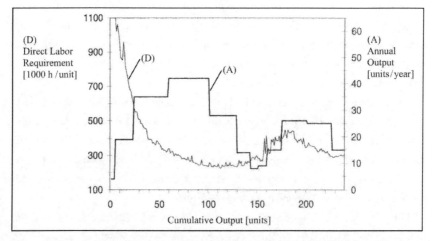

Figure 4: Direct Labor Requirement and Annual Output for Lockheed L1011 Aircraft Production (Benkard, 2000)

Economic Characteristics of Aerospace Organizations 17

The organizational *learning effect* takes into account the diminishing effort that is required for manufacture of follow-on units under the same quality standards. Aircraft production is driven by strong learning effects (Wright, 1936). The learning rate p, an indicator for learning effect, varies across each plane type (Alchian, 1963) and depends on the number n of units built (Arend, 1987). This can be set, in the case of continuous production, if no other data are available, to the following values (Goehlich, 2002): p = 0,90 for n = 2 to 100 units built, p = 0,95 for n = 101 to 1000 units built, and p = 1,00 for n > 1000 or n = 1 units built. Thus, p is diminishing with an increase in units built. Learning primarily results from process improvements and same task repetition: economists and engineers analyze the production process and make small changes that result in gradual productivity improvements. The use of new technologies allows processes to require less manpower. Workers become more efficient at the tasks they perform through multiple repetitions. It should be noted that learning comes at high costs too. Same task repetition is the result of process improvements and planning of the company's organizational structure. New technologies must be studied, verified in experiments and implemented. These activities require manpower resources, expensive labor experiments and acquisitions. This means that a reduction in direct labor requirements is also the result of expenditures (the program improvement budget), which must be taken into account. It can be said that total necessary development costs are divided into non-recurring costs (before the start of production) and into recurring costs (during production). Consequently, as Benkard (2004) claims, is "direct labor requirements" per unit the correct parameter to assess the learning effect? I suggest that the parameter would be better defined as "direct labor requirements plus program improvement budget" per unit in order to correctly model coherences (see Thompson, 2001).

The organizational *forgetting effect* is the hypothesis that a companies' stock of production experience depreciates over time (Argote, Beckman & Epple, 1990). This is caused by the turnover and worker layoffs that embody company experiences. One reason for depreciation of experience occurs in times of falling production rates because those times are accompanied by layoffs. During subsequent increases in production, the company is often unable to acquire the same workers that it formerly released and must retain entirely new workers (Benkard, 2000). In today's aerospace business, whether industry or government, it is common that a substantial number of employees are hired as contract workers in addition to the organization's permanent staff. The motivation for this is to easily dismiss employees in times where fewer laborers are needed. Another incentive is to evade (bureaucratic) requirements. Due to political and organizational reasons that require maintenance of the balance of power allocations, each division is strictly limited in its number of permanent staff, but lesser regulation exists concerning the number of contract workers allowed. Organizational forgetting is also caused by shifting employees to another division or by the normal rates of employee turnover during periods of constant production. It can be assumed that with the increasing size of an organization, the forgetting effect becomes stronger because more requirements exist and the probability that employees are shifted to another division wherein they cannot use their existing knowledge is high. It is very difficult to identify organizational forgetting, however, because data could be consistent, with either a 20% learning rate or a 25% learning rate with 5% forgetting (Benkard, 2000).

c) Operation Phase

In the case of the Space Shuttle, it has been planned to have a simple operation with a high flight rate, as shown in Figure 5 (left). The reality is that doing so requires a complex operation, as shown in Figure 5 (right) for this transportation system with a low flight rate of a few launches per year, and total costs are approximately $0,5 billion per flight. Why do cases like this (the Space Shuttle, for example) occur? Cases such as these can be explained by combining three negative (economic) factors with the (technical) factor that aerospace technology is typically very challenging: a trade-off dilemma, a business proposal dilemma and a budget cut dilemma.

Figure 5: Vision Versus Reality of Space Shuttle Operation (NASA, 2000b)

Economic Characteristics of Aerospace Organizations 19

One of the most controversial topics is the *trade-off dilemma* that exists between development and operation costs: if more effort (in particular in the form of monetary value) is invested in development, operation costs decrease and vice versa. Simplified, decision-makers can select between two program scenarios. Scenario A: low development costs in the short-term (next 10 years) and high operation costs in the long-term (10 to 40 years later). Scenario B: high development costs in the short-term (next 10 years) and low operation costs in the long-term (10 to 40 years later). Rational thinking decision-makers have an incentive to choose Scenario A because the award system (career, salary, bonus, etc.) awards only short-term successes, but not long-term successes.

Next, the *business proposal dilemma* is discussed. To win a business proposal, an incentive exists to estimate "Ideal Cost," which assumes that everything goes as planned (standard industrial proposal) resulting in low cost assumptions: an asset when competing for a contract. However, the history of rocketry teaches differently. In particular, for the space sector, estimated concept life-cycle costs are typically only a fraction of actual, realized space system costs. Technology challenges are more demanding than often assumed and time passes more quickly than planned. For example, the Space Shuttle orbiter development schedule was extended by 20%, which resulted in increased costs of 22%, while the orbiter experienced 25% mass growth during development, which resulted in lower payload performance (NASA, 2000a).

Finally, the *budget cut dilemma* is introduced. During the term of a program, budget cuts commonly occur due to political reorganization if governmentally funded, or due to market shifting if privately funded. Typically, a large number of aerospace programs are government funded and thus, this topic is of major importance. However, one of the least well-understood sources of instability is the political domain. Overnight, new policies can restrict the launch of vehicles or can revise budgets lower, which can force dramatic change in project scope or even cancellation of aerospace programs. For example, in 1997, 32% of US defense programs experienced budget reductions by Congress, 53% experienced budget increases and only 15% received the budget they requested (Weigel & Hastings, 2004). It can be concluded that the probability that a budget will change is much larger than the probability that it will remain on a nominal path. For an aerospace program to be robust, it must successfully endure any changes that may occur during the course of development and operation. Understanding the effects of political domain instabilities in the form of uncertain future annual budgets on aerospace programs is, therefore, of major importance.

2.2.7 Performance

Measuring the performance of aerospace organizations is a challenge, because there are often many indicators and various viewpoints. Table 7 shows the world's leading aerospace companies ranked by revenue, a common performance indicator. As a result of their survey, Woo and Willard (1983) identify 14 distinct indicators to evaluate (strategic) performance: Return on Investment, Return on Sales, Growth in Revenue, Cash Flow/Investment, Market Share, Market Share Gain, Product Quality Relative to Competitors, New Product Activities Relative to Competitors, Direct Cost Relative to Competitors, Product R&D, Process R&D, Variation in ROI, Percentage Point Change in ROI and Percentage Point Change in Cash Flow/Investment.

However, high performance is not always an organization's primary objective. Most aerospace companies' military business comes from government contracts that do not provide incentives for operating efficiently. In addition, most military products are not part of a free market economy due to the government's separation from the private sector. Even if high performance is the primary objective, it may be limited by external factors. Political restrictions can make it impossible to sell businesses that lose money due to unemployment effects. Shareholder restrictions can force companies to maintain duplicative facilities or top management positions, as in the case of EADS (Anselmo, 2005). Low performance can be commonly due to learning effects; aviation companies price their aircraft well below static marginal costs, which is inconsistent with static profit maximization, but consistent with dynamic profit maximization (Benkard, 2004).

Table 7: Aerospace Companies Ranked by Revenue (based on: Anselmo, 2005)

Rank	Name	2003 Revenue [billion $]
1	Boeing	51,5
2	EADS	43,3
3	United Technologies	37,0
4	Lockheed Martin	35,5
5	Northrop Grumman	29,9
6	Honeywell International	25,6
7	Raytheon	20,2
8	General Dynamics	19,2
9	BAE Systems	17,5
10	Bombardier	15,7

2.3 Discussion

For each characteristic introduced in this study, I choose the key points (shown in the headline), which are, in my opinion, worthy of discussion. I compare these points to other industry sectors, trends taken from the literature and/or my own assessment.

- **Market Structure: Few space organizations have significant market power**
  As learned from the characteristic "Market Structure," the space market is dominated by only a few space organizations. Here, market power is defined as the ability of organizations to price above marginal cost.

- **Products: Highly complex systems**
  As it can be surmised from the "Products" characteristic, aerospace products are highly complex and require significant engineering, manufacturing and supply chain management capabilities, as confirmed by A.T. Kearney (2003). For example, an airplane can comprise up to six million parts, whereas a car may consist of only some 7000 parts. Thus, life-cycle times in aerospace (sometimes more than 25 years) are dramatically longer than for the automotive industry (3-6 years).

- **Contractor Classification: High outsourcing ratio trend**
  The characteristic "Contractor Classification" indicates that there is a trend for outsourcing higher ratios and larger units. Larger sub-assemblies or systems come into the final airplane assembly line rather than components and smaller sub-assemblies that require scheduling and inventory management, as has been done in past. This significantly reduces the overall final assembly time and materials management, as stated by Slansky (2005).

- **Industry Size: High national security demands create a large military market share**
  As shown in the characteristic "Industry Size" section, the military's share of the aerospace industry is about half of the total sector's revenue. Thus, the aerospace business is driven not only by economic aspects, but also strongly by national security demands. Therefore, aerospace is a highly politicized sector (McGuire, 2006). For example, the US government is currently operating under a restrictive launch

policy; the American space transportation policy of 1994 requires US government payloads to fly on US-launched vehicles (The White House, 2006). As a result, similar key technologies have been developed individually, wherein each country maintains its own research budget, but with similar objectives. The result is an over-supply of more or less similar national rockets on the one hand and limited demand due to a stagnant satellite market, on the other hand.

- **Organizational Architecture: Highly necessary efforts are partly compensated by strong government financial support**
  The characteristic "Organizational Architecture" shows that developing, producing and operating aerospace products is quite tricky. For example, the aerospace sector is marked in the literature by very high fixed costs in the form of plant and research costs (McGuire, 2006), high financial risks (beta values typically reach 1,8 for de-regulated commercial airlines (Mullins, 1982)), low profit margins (lower than 5% is the rule (Lynn, 1998)) and very long payback periods (Sherry & Sarsfield, 2002). In the past, governments have played a leading role in the funding of the aerospace sector's research and capital-intensive infrastructure (The White House, 2000). I ex-pect a continuation in government subsidization of the aerospace sector due to the low return on research investments, on the one hand, and the government's high in-terest in aerospace, on the other hand.

- **Performance: Challenging assessment of performance**
  As mentioned in the characteristic "Performance" section, it is hard to assess per-formance. Performance should not only be expressed in terms of profitability, be-cause profitability alone, as an indicator for performance, would cause misalign-ment. An organization must also balance the competing claims of its various stake-holders, in addition to focusing on the welfare of stockholders, to ensure their con-tinuing cooperation, as argued by Barnard (1938). For example, most aerospace product lines are not profitable, i.e., manufacturers rely on one or two hugely suc-cessful products to positively affect their portfolio (McGuire, 2006). However, without its unprofitable product lines, companies may not be competitive in the market, because, for example, airline customers are typically attracted by a family aircraft concept.

2.4 Results

The purpose of this study is to investigate the characteristics of aerospace organizations, focusing primarily on two sectors: aviation and space. The aerospace sector has many unique characteristics when compared with "normal" businesses. Unique characteristics identified in this study are: high market power for some types of organizations, highly complex systems, high outsourcing ratio trends, large military market shares, strong governmental financial support and challenging assessment of performance.

Further, this study offers the idea that the aviation and space sectors are, for many features (e.g., high quality standards, massive entry costs, very low production rates, high strategic power and high degree of internationalization) nearly identical, while for other features (e.g., market structure, demand-supply interactions, unit size of production and imperfect competition) different.

Other extreme sectors also exist, such as the oil rig sector, the World Wide Web sector, the shipbuilding sector, and so on, that have unique and partly similar characteristics to the aerospace sector. An investigation into those sectors is not within the scope of the present study, but may be a fruitful area for future research.

3 Outsourcing Strategies in Europe, USA and Japan: A Case of Space Organizations

This chapter investigates the advantages of outsourcing versus vertical integration in three geographical areas. In the first section, I briefly review the literature on classic organizational theories concerning outsourcing. These theories form the foundation for developing my three hypotheses, as found in section two. To verify the hypotheses, I apply them to a case study, as described in section three. Section four follows with a discussion that includes the limitations of my study and offers a path for future research. The chapter concludes with speculation on the practical value of economic theory in general, vis-à-vis space organizations' outsourcing decisions.

3.1 Introduction

In this research, I focus on space organizations in three geographic areas: Japan, Europe and the USA. Space organizations were originally set up as governmental entities for exploration and for the commercial use of space, which can include research, development and operation of rockets and satellites, manned missions, and so on. For Europe, I include ESA (European Space Agency), for the USA, I use NASA (National Aeronautics and Space Administration) and for Japan, I focus on JAXA (Japan Aerospace Exploration Agency). Special attention is given to JAXA, as this organization is currently in the privatization process. It has been noted that "The (Japanese) government is now following a policy of privatization of the space industry, for example JAXA is outsourcing some of its maintenance activities to private companies and is trying also to increase revenues through its operations" (Polak & Belmondo, 2006, p. 24).

To understand this move, one needs to recall some recent events. The optimistic commercial satellite market environment of the 1990s has presently led to an overcapacity in the launch services industry. The projected future growth convinced many launch service providers to invest in new or upgraded launch vehicles, such as the Delta IV, Ariane 5 ECA and the H-IIA (Hague, 2003).

Some sort of rationalization, therefore, became necessary in order to stabilize this industry in the current market environment, especially since a break-even point in the commercial satellite market is years away (Hague, 2003). This is one of the key aspects related to why JAXA is in the process of outsourcing its commercial launcher operations. In addition, JAXA is also considering expanding Japan's role in the commercial launch services world market, following an impressive record of 12 out of 13 successful launches into orbit (Asahi Shinbun, 15 September 2007).

In recent decades, outsourcing has become a major issue in the economic field of research. Companies have the choice of whether to outsource activities or integrate them vertically. In the case of outsourcing activities, there is a shift of production and/or services to other companies.

The advantages of outsourcing result through several phenomena (Brickley, Smith & Zimmerman, 2006): (1) New and more flexible production technologies allow suppliers to adapt easily to customer demands. This technical development leads to less firm-specific assets. (2) Improved communication technologies make daily operations easier. As an example of this, one can observe speedy inventory ordering by suppliers through the use of computers. (3) Increased globalization has led to pressure on many firms to reduce costs and to increase their efficiency. (4) Excess capacities enable firms to obtain discounts from suppliers. This can be caused by worldwide or geographically restricted recessions.

Another phenomenon in regards to governmental organizations is the shortage of finance. A country in high deficit might be more willing to outsource public projects to private companies. Even in countries like Germany, one can see these developments. These savings can be seen in the bus transport industry, where in recent years more and more bus lines have either been closed or switched over to private companies. All of these phenomena can be seen as reasons for forcing companies to undertake outsourcing.

The three areas of investigation differ with respect to their market basis. There is, at least in Anglo-Saxon countries, an unspoken agreement that the maximization of shareholder value is the most relevant objective (Rappaport, 1986). In contrast, Japan and also Europe can be considered as quite different from this Anglo-Saxon approach. Therefore, the interest of this research lies in the differences found among all three areas.

3.2 Theoretical Approaches for Outsourcing

3.2.1 General

I employ three theoretical approaches for outsourcing in space organizations: transaction cost theory, agency theory and the human resource-based view. I will show what specific trade-off exists between vertical integration and outsourcing, and formulate my own hypothesis based on theory's prediction for space organization activity. Finally, I verify this hypothesis for the space organization case study.

3.2.2 Transaction Cost Theory

One of the widely accepted concepts for measuring outsourcing is transaction cost theory, based on the work of Coase (1937). According to Coase, transactions should be organized within a company as long as the costs of these transactions are lower than the transaction costs in the market. Transaction costs include searching, contracting, controlling, recontracting and the risk of delays for both sides.

On behalf of transaction cost theory, all parties use information according to their advantages, which leads to a strategic asymmetry. To make it simple: a seller attempts to hide negative product characteristics and a buyer does not show his upper limit for purchasing a given product. This leads to each party investing in information costs, as both are trying to receive more and better information. A seller might be interested in undertaking market research about his customers' behavior. A buyer, on the other hand, might be interested in testing a product before buying it. In the literature, there are several attempts to overcome these contracting difficulties (Akerlof, 1970).

The transaction cost concept is the predominant theoretical explanation in management studies and basically sets out to explain governance choices and ex-post contractual costs (Williamson, 1975). This theoretical concept is widely used for its analytical rigor but is also criticized for overemphasizing ex-post contractual influences and underemphasizing revenue creation (White, 2000).

In sum, transaction cost theory suggests that outsourcing should be considered if activities: (1) do not require investments in specific assets that invite hold-up; (2) are not subject to a high degree of environmental uncertainty; and (3) are those activities which the organization infrequently relies upon (Aubert, Rivard & Patry, 1996; Masten, 1984). In the following case of space organizations, this industry can be characterized by a high level of uncertainty (few satellite customers dictate world market demand), with very specific assets (launchers, launch operation facilities, and so on), and who frequently rely on those assets (main part of revenue and public acceptance comes from successful launches). This leads me to the first hypothesis, as stated below.

Hypothesis 1: In accordance with transaction cost theory, the outsourcing activities of space organizations would result in higher transaction costs than would vertical integration activities, especially when there is a high uncertainty environment, very specific assets and high frequency use.

Nevertheless, in the following case of space organizations, companies increasingly outsource those activities that are in contradiction to the central tenets of transaction cost theory. This leads to the assumption that transaction cost theory has a minor influence on organizational decisions compared to agency theory, the human resource-based view, and other theories. Another explanation could be that some companies or space organizations might not be able to produce certain products or use certain technologies on their own. In this case, an outsourcing of its own activities might be unavoidable. A further reason is that reputation and repetition provide a strong incentive to the operator for providing excellent service. For example, a launch failure caused by the operator may have irreparable damage for its brand image (i.e., reputation) and may lead to no further orders being placed with the operator (i.e., repetition).

3.2.3 Principal-Agent Theory

Another dominant conceptual framework is the agency concept. The idea of the agency concept goes back to Jensen and Meckling (1976), who described the relationship between principals and agents. Principals rely on agents who carry out what the principals want them to do. The agent might be a CEO whose own interests are not automatically in line with the interests of the principal (e.g., the shareholder of the company). Worth mentioning are Holmstrom's various investigations in such models (e.g., Holmstrom, 1999). In order to attain equilibrium, agency theory emphasizes the cost of misalignment between principals and agents (Becht, Bolton & Roell, 2003). Potential misalignment conflicts arise between a principal and an agent, thus causing economic costs (Jensen & Meckling, 1976).

In sum, one main aspect of principal-agent theory defines a trade-off between the costs for the principal of monitoring outsourced activities, such as parts, products and human resources, in order to achieve the main goal of the principal (i.e., a cost increase) and the benefit of less organizational effort due to fewer interactions (i.e., a cost reduction). Space organizations consist, in the following case, as the principal, while companies to which activities are outsourced are the agents. Due to relatively high failure rates, the operation of launchers is very risky, so outsourcing would be an advantage for the space organization. As effective quality standards and processes exist in the aerospace sector, monitoring costs caused by outsourcing would be moderate. This leads me to the second hypothesis, as stated below.

Hypothesis 2: According to agency theory, outsourcing activities for space organizations would be preferable over vertical integration when the costs of misalignment conflicts caused by outsourcing are lower than the costs of the incentive provisions caused by vertical integration.

This hypothesis is in correlation with the following case of space organizations. It requires relatively little effort to "monitor" a launch operator compared to other services. Risk transferring to the launch operator is high facilitation for space organizations; delays, launch failures and succession failure investigations within the organization can harm a large, clumsy bureaucratic space organization much more than a small and efficiently structured private launch operator. Another factor is that agents in a company have more incentive to work hard than in a government agency because their effort has more influence on their payoffs, e.g., salary, job guarantee, awards, and so on (Schmidt, 1996). Also, the soft budget constraints theory explains this effect by the fact that governments are sometimes forced to subsidize a government entity when it performs inefficiently, as while a bankruptcy may not be a credible threat to governmental bureaucrats, it certainly is to managers.

3.2.4 The Human Resource-based View

Another theoretical explanation for outsourcing and vertical integration is the human resource-based view. According to the human resource-based view, organizations differ in their use of human resources (Wernerfelt, 1984). Organizations with superior human

30   Outsourcing Strategies in Europe, USA and Japan: A Case of Space Organizations

resources can establish competitive advantages that enable them to outperform their rivals (Peteraf, 1993).

In sum, the human resource-based view recommends keeping strategic and competitive activities in-house, because the loss of human resource knowledge cannot be compensated by the increase in short-term financial advantages over the long run. This is an important aspect, particularly in the following case involving space organizations, as these companies are more specialized. Therefore, in these organizations, human resources are often critical because they cannot easily be replicated. This leads me to the third hypothesis, as stated below.

Hypothesis 3: The human resource-based view suggests that advantages accrue for space organizations that efficiently vertically integrate their activities, because outsourcing activities could lead to a loss of human resource knowledge.

Controversially, in all three investigated areas the respective space organizations outsource their strategic and competitive launch activities to a large extent, thus resulting in a major contradiction with the central tenets of the human resource-based view. This leads to the assumption that the human resource-based view has only a minor influence on organizational decisions compared to other theories in these cases. Another explanation might be that if space organizations are not able to provide their own human resources (i.e., specialists for imperative tasks are unavailable), an outsourcing of certain specific activities might be unavoidable.

3.3   Case Study of Space Organizations

3.3.1   General

In the following section, I introduce the case of space organizations from Europe, the USA and Japan to which I have applied the previously described theories. Ranking the world's space agencies in terms of annual total cash budget size in fiscal year 2006, NASA has the largest budget with around $16 billion, followed by Europe's ESA with a budget of about $3,8 billion and the Japanese JAXA budget of about $2,1 billion. The Chinese Space Agency (CSA) has a budget of around $1,3 billion, the Russian Space

Agency (RSA) around $1,2 billion and the Indian Space Research Organization (ISRO) has around $1,2 billion. One interesting aspect concerning the Chinese and Indian space programs is that their budgets are growing rapidly, largely as a result of the high growth rates of their domestic economies. The opposite development can be seen in Russia, where the space program has recently experienced severe budget constraints.

For the purpose of the specific investigation in this study, I will narrow the case study to the three big players in this field: Europe, the USA and Japan. Table 8 illustrates the space market structures of Europe, the USA and Japan for commercial launchers. The names of the organizations given in brackets are the major players, while minor players are not listed. The different life-cycle phases are explained in the following paragraphs.

Table 8: Comparison of Space Market Structures for Commercial Launchers

Life-cycle	Europe	USA	Japan
Basic Research/ Concept/ Definition	Government (ESA)	Government (NASA)	Government (JAXA)
Development/ Production	Private (EADS)	Private (Boeing)	Private (IHI, MHI)
Operation	Private (Arianespace)	Private (Boeing Launch Services)	Government (JAXA) *currently in process* Private (H-IIA Launch Services)
	since 1980	since 2001	since 2007

- **Basic Research, Concept and Definition Phases:** Typically, space agencies are responsible for the basic research phase. Basic research includes any fundamental research, which need not necessarily be related to a specific rocket program, such as investigations on novel propellants. Such studies are sometimes investigated over several decades. The concept phase includes preparation of a conceptual design and a system analysis. These activities are sometimes delegated to a consulting company. During the concept phase, system specifications, an assessment of political restrictions and advanced development on high-risk items (e.g., rocket engines) are completed. The concept and definition phase can usually be accomplished within 5 years.

- **Development and Production Phase:** Typically, private companies develop and produce the rocket. The development phase refers to the complete development of the rocket, including tests on one or more prototypes and construction of ground support if not yet existing from older rocket programs. This phase can be accomplished within 4 to 6 years. Normally, prototype flights are used to transport scientific satellites into space. If the test flights are successful, the series production of that rocket starts.

- **Operation Phase:** For early commercial space flights, space agencies were responsible for the operation and marketing of launchers. Later on, some space agencies outsourced those tasks to launch service companies. In Europe, the world's first launch service company was created in 1980, and the USA followed in 2001. Japan is currently in the process of privatizing the operation of launchers.

3.3.2 Europe

The major players for the commercial launcher sector in Europe are ESA for research, EADS for development and production, and Arianespace for operation.

a) Governmental Key Leaders (Research)

The European Space Agency (ESA), established in 1975, consists of 17 member states. The ESA falls roughly within the geographical scope of the European Union (EU); however, Switzerland and Norway are also member states and there is strong cooperation with Canada. A long-term goal for the ESA is to attract all EU states to become members by 2014 (ESA, 2006). The ESA has a staff of about 1900 employees with an annual budget of about $3,8 billion in 2006. The three largest contributors are France (about 30%), Germany (about 25%) and Italy (about 15%).

b) Private Key Leaders (Development & Production)

EADS was formed by its member companies in July 2000, becoming the world's second largest aerospace company after Boeing. One of its divisions, Astrium, with its subsidiary EADS Astrium Transportation, is a prime contractor for the Ariane 5 launcher. This company developed the Ariane launcher family, and is responsible for the delivery to Arianespace of a complete and completely tested launcher while managing all contracts associated with its manufacturers. Member states, through the ESA, fund the development costs for the Ariane launchers and the associated technology. The company has facilities in France (Les Mureaux near Paris and Aquitaine near Bordeaux) and Germany (Bremen). In 2006, the space division had a workforce of about 11 000 employees and consolidated revenues of $4,4 billion, representing 12% of EADS' total revenues (EADS, 2007).

c) Private Key Leaders (Operation)

Arianespace is a commercial launch service operator, holding more than 50% of the world market for satellites destined for Geostationary Transfer Orbit (GTO). Created as the first commercial space transportation company in 1980, Arianespace has signed contracts for 280 satellite payloads. About 270 employees work for this company. Arianespace has 23 shareholders including the French space agency CNES with 34% and EADS with 30%, while all of the European companies participate in the construction of the Ariane launchers (Arianespace, 2007). Although it operates as a private firm, Arianespace receives considerable, although indirect, support from the European Space Agency, which purchases Arianespace's launch services.

3.3.3 USA

The major players for the commercial launcher sector in the USA are NASA for research, Boeing for development and production, and Boeing Launch Services for operation.

a) Governmental Key Leaders (Research)

The National Aeronautics and Space Administration (NASA) is the agency responsible for the nation's public space program. It had a budget of around $16 billion in 2006. NASA conducts its work in four principle organizations, called mission directorates: aeronautics, exploration systems, science operations and space operations. The Space Operations Mission Directorate provides critical enabling technologies for much of NASA through the Space Shuttle, the International Space Station and flight support (NASA, 2006).

b) Private Key Leaders (Development & Production)

Boeing operates in four principal segments: Commercial Airplanes, Military Aircraft and Missile Systems, as well as in Space & Communications, and also in the so-called Boeing Capital Corporation. Space & Communications operations, with its Network & Space Systems Division, principally focuses on research, development and the production of space systems, missile defense systems, satellites, launch vehicles and rocket engines, and also the Space Shuttle and International Space Station (ISS) programs (Boeing, 2008). In 2006, the Network & Space Systems Division's revenues were $12 billion, representing 20% of Boeing's total revenues (Boeing, 2007b). Boeing has developed and continues to produce the Delta launcher family. The company has customers in more than 90 countries around the world and is one of the largest US exporters in terms of sales. Recently, Boeing started to shift its core business away from commercial aircraft manufacturing toward space vehicles, communications, technical services and defense applications (MacPherson & Pritchard, 2002).

c) Private Key Leaders (Operation)

Boeing Launch Services (BLS), which is based in Huntington Beach, USA, is an organization that combines strategic planning, business development and sales for commercial launch service customers. It is a wholly owned subsidiary of Boeing and is part of Boeing's Integrated Defense Systems. BLS markets the Sea Launch and Delta IV launcher family (Boeing, 2008).

3.3.4 Japan

The major players for the commercial space launch sector in Japan are JAXA for research, Ishikawajima Heavy Industries (IHI) and Mitsubishi Heavy Industries (MHI) for development and production, and H-IIA Launch Services for operation launches.

a) Governmental Key Leaders (Research)

JAXA is the result of the merge between the National Space Development Agency of Japan (NASDA), the National Aerospace Laboratory of Japan (NAL), and the Institute of Space and Astronautical Science (ISAS) in 2003. JAXA went through a drastic reduction of staff, and more focus has since been put on the ISS program. JAXA now follows a policy of privatization, which can be observed from various documented sources,

Outsourcing Strategies in Europe, USA and Japan: A Case of Space Organizations　35

such as "Take steps toward turning the space equipment industry and the space utilization service industry into the key industries of Japan," as described in JAXA's Vision 2025 (JAXA, 2005, p. 24).

b) Private Key Leaders (Development & Production)

The key companies involved in the development and production of commercial launchers in Japan are Mitsubishi Heavy Industries for liquid-fueled rockets (e.g., the main stage of H-IIA), IHI for the upper stages and small engines, and Nissan for the solid fuelled rockets (e.g., strap-on boosters of H-IIA). Typically, these companies have in-house R&D groups that co-develop programs with JAXA, while privately financed R&D programs are almost non-existent in Japan (Polak & Belmondo, 2006).

c) Governmental / Private Key Leaders (Operation)

H-IIA Launch Services, as organized by Mitsubishi Heavy Industries, is Japan's newly established launch operator resulting from the privatization process of H-IIA launch operations initiated in 2002. The H-IIA No. 13 rocket, launched in September 2007, was the first H-IIA to be launched after JAXA's privatization program (Asahi Shinbun, 15 September 2007). H-IIA Launch Services promotes the sales and marketing of launch operations to governmental and commercial customers all over the world. Furthermore, it offers support services that are normally performed by the customers themselves, including the pre-launch operation and safety checks of spacecraft at Tanegashima Space Center, arrangement for launch-related insurance, re-launch, back-up launch and finance (Mitsubishi Heavy Industries, 2007).

3.4　Discussion

3.4.1　General

The given case study has been examined using the three separate theories discussed in previous sections. In the following section, this investigation will attempt to widen the point of view through a discussion centered on the coherences, alternatives and limitations concerning the applied theories.

3.4.2 Understanding of Coherences

As I stated in Hypothesis 1, the outsourcing activities of the Japanese JAXA are hard to explain using transaction cost theory. Also, the human resource-based view, represented by Hypothesis 3, carries little support. Only agency theory holds, represented by Hypothesis 2, as it can be applied to the privatization of the operational part of the JAXA space organization.

As I stated in Hypothesis 3, outsourcing is normally connected to a loss of knowledge, which is problematic in the area of human resources. What can be seen in space organizations is that several space organizations outsource specific production assets. However, the research part is normally covered by the space organizations themselves. Therefore, space organizations seem to benefit from outsourcing certain activities, while others are kept within the organization. Another factor is that the vertical integration of activities is mainly used in basic research sectors where it is not profitable to outsource activities.

The aim of JAXA is to increase the competitiveness of Japanese commercial launch services. To do so, JAXA needs to reduce costs, increase reliability and improve customer service. In sum, I argue that, under the current organizational architecture (i.e., where basic research, production and operating divisions are vertically integrated), the ability of this organization to increase its commercial competitiveness is significantly limited. The reason for this is that an efficient organizational architecture is different for a basic research division and an operation division: While, for example, in a basic research division the reward system needs to be optimized to elicit innovations from scientists, the reward system in an operation division needs to be optimized to motivate managers to create lean processes and high quality standards.

3.4.3 Alternative Theories

I selected three theories out of a pool of alternatives because I expect that they are best suited for my investigation centered on outsourcing strategies, while also providing me with some significant results within the respective frameworks of transaction cost theory, agency theory and the human resource-based view.

I am aware that there are other theories or approaches, e.g., the property rights theory, which posit that outsourcing stimulates efficient bargaining power (see Grossman & Hart, 1986). Also, rent-seeking theory as a concept can be discussed in this area. According to rent-seeking theory, vertical integration can stop socially destructive haggling over appropriate quasi-rents (see Williamson, 1985), but vertical integration does not completely eliminate contracting problems (Klein, Crawford & Alchian, 1978). For instance, influence activities (giving someone authority means that this person will be lobbied) subsequently results in high costs (Milgrom & Roberts, 1988). Finally, adaptation theory also exists, which stipulates that owning an asset allows the owner to determine how the asset is consequently used (see Williamson, 1975).

3.4.4 Limitations

Generally, the weakness of these theories is that they make speculative assumptions about human cognition and managerial discretion (Mahnke, 2001). Managers who need to decide on whether to vertically integrate or to outsource tasks are usually faced with a general lack of relevant information. This fact strengthens the bounded rationality, which means that human actors involved in complex problem solving are limited in knowledge, skills and time (Cyert & March, 1963). Instead, managers are driven by means of an experimental search to discover possibilities for improving the efficiency of the organization.

Another weakness of these theories is their limitations of scope. Essentially, transaction cost theory is restricted to the issue of the costs of writing complete contracts, while principal-agent theory narrowly focuses on the issue of moral hazard, and the human resource-based view is limited to the simple issue of linking resources to property.

Finally, it should be noted that outsourcing by companies and governments has similar but not completely identical objectives. Typically, the company's motivation is based mainly on economical aspects, while the government's motivation might also be based on political aspects. Furthermore, my definition of outsourcing is always connected to switching from governmental activities to private companies. Overall, this kind of outsourcing is much stronger than from one private to another private company.

3.5 Results

In this chapter, I explore a number of reasons why the Japanese government's space organization, JAXA, recently intensified its outsourcing activities to private companies.

This process is shown to have occurred several years ago in the other investigated areas: Europe and the USA.

The directional trend of outsourcing activities in space organizations, therefore, is most congruent with principal-agent theory. In contrast, transaction cost theory and the human resource-based view both fail to provide sufficient reasons to explain why JAXA should vertically integrate its activities to be more efficient, rather than outsourcing them to private companies.

I also conclude that economic theories can be used for a wide field of industrial sectors, but have limited use with regard to the space sector. One reason for this might be that the characteristics of aerospace organizations, and in particular space organizations, are unique as compared to the overall characteristics of most other industries, as shown in Chapter 2.

4 Development of a Make-or-Buy Decision-supporting Process

The objective of this chapter is to analyze and support the make-or-buy decision. This is realized by the development of a theory-based decision process. In this study, the process is applied to aerospace organizations as a tool, but its transparency and modularization enables the process to be applied to any organization of interest. The chapter is structured as follows. In the next section, the make-or-buy continuum philosophy is introduced. In section two, the literature is qualitatively reviewed by presenting the pros and cons concerning vertical integration and outsourcing. For illustration, the tool's propositions are supplemented with examples taken from the aerospace sector. Then, those pros and cons are quantitatively assessed and ranked by importance and probability. Next, the developed process is applied to four case studies. Finally, section three offers a discussion of sensitivity analysis, comparison with other studies and limitations.

4.1 Introduction

A company has many architectural choices from which to produce its products or services (Figure 6). At one extreme, the product or service can be purchased from any supplier in the spot market. At the other extreme, the company can produce the product or service internally within a division. Between the extremes are various long-term contracts, such as strategic alliances, franchise agreements, lease contracts, joint ventures and supply contracts (Brickley, Smith & Zimmerman, 2006). Note that a certain overlap exists between different types of long-term contracts and typology can vary in some buyer-supplier relationships.

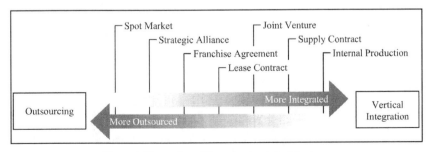

Figure 6: Illustration of Organizational Architectures

Outsourcing is derived from the English language and is a neologism of the words "outsider-resource-using," which means that the responsibility for resources is shifted to third parties (Płaczek & Szołtysek, 2006). In the literature, the term outsourcing is widely understood to be the process of moving an activity that was formerly finalized "completely inside" the organization to one in which the activity is finalized "completely outside" the organization.

In this study, however, the terms outsourcing and vertical integration are seen relatively, not absolutely. Here, organizational architectures are processed between two extremes: outsourcing means to move an activity "more outside" the company, while vertical integration means to move an activity "more inside" the company. For example, a change from a joint venture to a lease contract is defined here as outsourcing because activities are relatively less vertically integrated in a lease contract than in a joint venture. Long-term contracts are introduced briefly, as follows:

- **Strategic Alliance:** Alliances, or constellations of bilateral agreements among companies, are increasingly necessary to successfully compete in today's global market. Strategic alliances are based on the exchange of hostages (e.g., surety bonds, exchange of debt or equity positions) and allow the development of long-term collaborative intentions that permit partners to meet strategic goals (Lau, 1994; Mattsson, 1995). Alliances are difficult to define because their structural characteristics are diverse. Japanese strategic alliances, e.g., operate in networks of relationships between companies based on long-term mutuality, rather than on clearly defined regulations or on inter-firm hierarchical organizational structures (Gerlach, 1997), as commonly practiced in Western countries. Tactical alliances (e.g., code-sharing agreements), which are loose forms of collaboration, and normally do not involve major resource commitments, are another form of strategic alliances (Bennett, 1997).

- **Franchise Agreement:** According to Todeva and Knoke (2005), franchising means that a franchiser (the buyer) grants a franchisee (the supplier) the use of a brand-name identity, but retains control over pricing, marketing and standardized service norms.

- **Lease Contract:** Leasing implies that one company grants another the right to use patented technologies or processes in return for royalties (Todeva & Knoke, 2005). In the literature (Miller & Upton, 1976), leasing is distinguished between short- and

Development of a Make-or-Buy Decision-supporting Process 41

long-term leases. Short-term leases are for the shortest practicable interval of time, e.g., three hours for renting a bicycle, one day for renting a car or several years for renting specialized industrial equipment. Long-term leases are used for an extension over more than a single period, e.g., several years for renting a copy machine.

- **Joint Venture:** Joint ventures involve two or more organizations, each of which shares in the decision-making activities, such as marketing or research and development (R&D), of the jointly owned entity (Geringer, 1988). Joint ventures with 50-50 ownership are common.

- **Supply Contract:** Suppliers can be distinguished into four categories (Kamath & Liker, 1994): (1) partner suppliers are jointly involved in specification writing from the beginning of the project; (2) mature suppliers wait for rough specifications from the buyer before they begin work; (3) subordinate suppliers manufacture based on detailed specifications given from the buyer; and (4) contractual suppliers propose standard parts that are available through a catalog.

4.2 The Process

4.2.1 General

The make-or-buy decision-supporting process is structured as shown in Figure 7 and comprises four submodules. The submodule "Settings" is illustrated in detail in Figure 8. This module processes the input data of strategic objectives, organizational characteristics, product characteristics and environmental characteristics. The module is based on a balanced scorecard philosophy, of which detailed information can be found in the discussion section of this study. The submodule "Integration Pros" processes the main advantages of vertical integration from the point of view of the final assembler (Figure 9), while the submodule "Outsourcing Pros" processes those advantages of outsourcing as shown in Figure 10. The submodule "Results" processes the output data as shown in Figure 11.

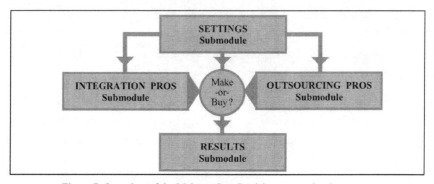

Figure 7: Overview of the Make-or-Buy Decision-supporting Process

SETTINGS Submodule		
Strategic Objectives	**Characteristics**	
Set01 Increase market share	**Organization Characteristics**	**Environment Characteristics**
Set02 Increase quality	Set07 Organization size	Set14 Intensity of competition
Set03 Increase stability	Set08 Technical experience	Set15 Market demand uncertainty
Set04 Increase short-term profit	Set09 Organizational skills	Set16 Quality of business climate
Set05 Increase flexibility	**Product Characteristics**	
Set06 Increase control	Set10 Product complexity	
	Set11 Asset specificity	
	Set12 Strategic vulnerability	
	Set13 Technology uncertainty	

Figure 8: Settings Submodule

Vertical integration and outsourcing propositions are divided into control, stability and coordination aspects. Control aspects are those that help the organization in terms of ease of monitoring, high transparency of processes, low opportunistic behaviors and low bureaucracy. In the group of stability aspects are those propositions that support the organization's existence, such as high quality, high protection of sensitive information, low risk and high flexibility. Coordination aspects comprise propositions that increase positive interactions, such as high organizational synergies, low costs and better strategy realization. The submodule "Results" presents the results of this process in the form of clear graphics.

The procedure for developing this process is completed in three steps. Step 1 is a qualitative assessment of the propositions that contribute to the make-or-buy decision. In this step, all propositions found by literature review are presented in the same format and are briefly discussed. Step 2 offers a quantitative assessment of those propositions, using Likert scaling, pairwise comparison and benefit estimation methods. Step 3 is an application of the process to aerospace organizations for verification and insight.

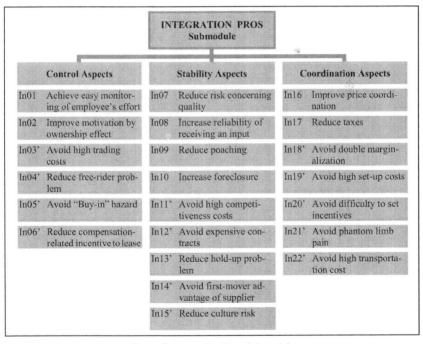

Figure 9: Integration Pros Submodule

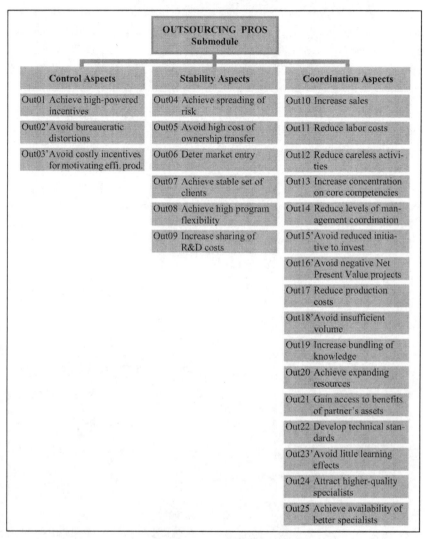

Figure 10: Outsourcing Pros Submodule

Development of a Make-or-Buy Decision-supporting Process   45

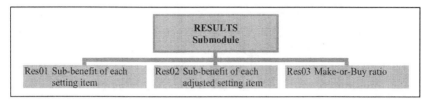

Figure 11: Results Submodule

4.2.2 Qualitative Assessment

Each submodule and its associated items, or propositions, is organized in the same manner for simple review. The "Settings" and "Results" submodule items are listed briefly, while the "Integration Pros" and "Outsourcing Pros" submodule propositions are listed in detail, as specified in the following text and shown by example in Figure 12. For reader-friendly use, all information is prepared in the same format.

In21' Avoid phantom limb pain

Description: Lost interaction effects with outsourced activities (independently on their core or non-core status) can diminish the effectiveness of the remaining activities (Mahnke, 2001).

Example: Airlines outsourced the handling of passenger luggage at airports. Even though airlines try to offer the best service for their first class passengers, the passenger satisfaction can be strongly blurred by dirty, damaged, delayed or lost luggage.

Solution: The organization can ensure that its remaining employees interact closely with its outsourced activities (Quinn & Hilmer, 1995). Alternatively, the organization can handle the "loss" better by finding and implementing alternatives, if the process of outsourcing is slower.

Figure 12: Example of a Vertical Integration Proposition

Header: The header is where I place the serial number and name of the proposition. As for the purpose of process development, I have reversed the propositions in such a way that the disadvantages of outsourcing become advantages of vertical integration and disadvantages of vertical integration become advantages of outsourcing. Those reversed propositions are marked with an apostrophe ('). Description: The description briefly introduces the proposition, but may also include additional information. Example: For illustration, each proposition is supplemented with an example taken from the aviation or space sector. Solution: Where appropriate, the solution paragraph presents suggestions for alternative countermeasures, in addition to the outsourcing or vertical integration philosophy. It becomes necessary to look at this fact when trading outsourcing for vertical integration. However, it should be mentioned that these countermeasures may yield high costs and realistically be used to certain intensity only.

---------------- *Description of items and propositions from here to page 72* ----------------

a) Settings Submodule (Strategic Objectives)

- **Set01 Increase market share (financial Key Performance Indicator (KPI))**
  Description: Market share indicates the percentage of sales in a given industry segment or sub-segment that are captured by the organization. This indicator has been widely used in the strategically-oriented literature and is stressed by PIMS (1977), for instance.
  Range: low = less than 30% share; high = greater than 70% share

- **Set02 Increase quality (customer KPI)**
  Description: Quality indicates the level of flawlessness of an activity and, when high, has a positive effect on customer satisfaction.
  Range: low = faulty; high = flawless

- **Set03 Increase stability (process KPI)**
  Description: Stability indicates the desired degree of risk avoidance. For example, leasing entails low levels of financial resource commitment, while integration reduces risks of technology plagiarism.
  Range: low = risk neutral, organization is not afraid to take chances and be fully responsible for any costs; high = risk averse, organization seeks to avoid risk

- **Set04 Increase short-term profit (financial KPI)**
  Description: Profit is a basic measure of the profitability of the organization and reveals the returns an organization can generate from creating and selling its products. Higher profits reflect greater efficiency in turning stock into income and larger

Development of a Make-or-Buy Decision-supporting Process 47

budgets available for reinvestment into the organization for research and development, marketing and other investments (Razvi, 2007).

Range: low = no profit; high = high profit

- **Set05 Increase flexibility (process KPI)**
  Description: Flexibility indicates the desired degree of ability to adapt organizational strategy to changing market conditions.
  Range: low = adaptation not possible or very costly; medium = adaptation possible, but costly; high = easy adaptation

- **Set06 Increase control (process KPI)**
  Description: Control indicates the desired degree of command power by management over activities.
  Range: low = no control; medium = partial control; high = full control

b) Settings Submodule (Organizational Characteristics)

- **Set07 Organization size (HR & innovation KPI)**
  Description: Size is an indicator of the organization's (human) resource availability. This indicator is most often interpreted as a source of organizational costs (Shepherd, 1972) because it is assumed to affect performance negatively (Rumelt, 1982).
  Range: low = a few hundred employees; medium = a few thousand employees; high = Large Scale Enterprise (LSE), over ten-thousand employees

- **Set08 Technical experience (HR & innovation KPI)**
  Description: Experience refers to the extent to which employees are involved and learn from similar products (Koelle, 2003).
  Range: low = new team with no relevant product experience; medium = some experience with related products; high = extensive experience with similar products

- **Set09 Organizational skills (HR & innovation KPI)**
  Description: Skills are an indicator of employee knowledge to coordinate projects and programs.
  Range: low = no project management experience; high = extensive project management experience

c) Settings Submodule (Product Characteristics)

- **Set10 Product complexity (process KPI)**

  Description: Complexity refers to the technical nature of the product.

  Range: low = simple unit; medium = connection of simple systems; high = connection and interaction of advanced systems

- **Set11 Asset specificity (process KPI)**

  Description: The degree of specificity for a certain activity is measured by the difference between the cost of the asset and the value of its second best use (Williamson, 1985).

  Range: low = reversible investment, e.g., capital expenditures; high = irreversible investment, e.g., knowledge acquisition

- **Set12 Strategic vulnerability (process KPI)**

  Description: The degree of vulnerability of strategic organizational development is measured by the amount the activity contributes to, or even represents, the organization's core competencies.

  Range: low = no relation to core competence; high = sensitive influence on core competences

- **Set13 Technology uncertainty (financial KPI)**

  Description: This indicator refers to the maturity level of technology used.

  Range: low = variation of existing design with minor modifications; medium = new design, but with existing components; high = first generation system with advanced state-of-the-art technology

d) Settings Submodule (Environmental Characteristics)

- **Set14 Intensity of competition (process KPI)**

  Description: This indicator refers to the number of competitors in the market.

  Range: low = no competitors, monopoly; medium = several competitors, oligopoly; high = many competitors, perfect competition

Development of a Make-or-Buy Decision-supporting Process

- **Set15 Market demand uncertainty (process KPI)**

  Description: This indicator includes unpredictable customer utilization, buying power, market seasons, standards, etc.

  Range: low = easy forecasting with no surprises; medium = challenging forecasting with some surprises; high = unforeseeable circumstances

- **Set16 Quality of business climate (HR & innovation KPI)**

  Description: The quality of a country's business climate is measured by the Business Environment Risk Index (BERI). BERI data is commercially available from Business Environment Risk Intelligence (2005). This data includes the following criteria with associated weights in brackets (Hollensen, 2007): political stability (12%), economic growth (10%), currency convertibility (10%), labor productivity (8%), short-term credit (8%), long-term loans (8%), attitude towards the foreign investor (6%), nationalization (6%), monetary inflation (6%), balance of payments (6%), enforceability of contracts (6%), bureaucratic delays (4%), communication infrastructure (4%), local management (4%) and services (2%). Estimating the values of these criteria leads to a sufficiently accurate indicator value for the purposes of this study.

  Range: low = unacceptable, very high risk; high = superior conditions, favorable environment for investors, advanced economy

e) Vertical Integration Pros Submodule (Control Aspects)

- **In01 Achieve easy monitoring of employee's effort**

  Description: An advantage of in-house production is the ability to monitor employee efforts compared to outsourcing, where the partner's activities normally take place in a legally distinct setting and generally geographically distinct location (Grossman & Helpman, 2004). Therefore, the likelihood of integration increases with the difficulty of monitoring performance (Anderson & Schmittlein, 1984). This argument holds for behavior monitoring. For outcome monitoring, vertical integration is not mandatory to achieve benefits in comparison with outsourcing.

  Example: In the aerospace industry, each task is detailed and described in the form of a contract, independently of whether or not the task is performed in-house or outsourced. Therefore, the potential for this argument is moderate.

- **In02 Improve motivation by ownership effect**

  Description: Ownership motivates the most productive investment decisions, e.g., house owners take better care of their living accommodations than renters (Smith & Wakeman, 1985).

  Example: Typically, as in many industry sectors, aerospace engineers have the opportunity to patent-register their ideas and concepts. They typically show high motivation to push their ideas forward, as incentives, such as monetary compensation, appreciation and self-realization, are concrete for "ownership ideas." The challenge for managers is to set incentives in such a way that engineers apply balanced effort distribution to all their tasks. See investigations on multitasks by Holmstrom and Milgrom (1991) for details.

- **In03' Avoid high trading costs**

  Description: Trading costs include ongoing costs for control and coordination, such as ordering, scheduling, monitoring progress and contract enforcement, in the case of outsourcing. As the frequency of transactions increase, vertical integration becomes more beneficial compared to outsourcing to keeping trading costs low (Williamson, 1985). The time and effort necessary to manage partnerships (ex-post) is generated by this typical kind of transaction cost perpetrator.

  Example: Boeing's relationship with its suppliers has been changing in recent years, as the company focuses on cutting costs and streamlining production. Boeing has been reducing the number of its suppliers and asking the remaining suppliers to produce larger assemblies, rather than individual parts (Wilhelm, 2001).

  Solution: Close geographical proximity between buyer and supplier plants facilitates coordination and communication.

- **In04' Reduce free-rider problem**

  Description: Companies have problems motivating independently owned (i.e., outsourced) retailers in a distribution system to invest in sufficient resources to maintain a brand name. Retailers have incentives to save costs by shirking on advertising and hiring less-skilled labor. All parties receive the benefits from cost reductions, but bear only part of the decline in sales, because these declines are shared with other units. In the case of outsourcing, shirking is easier than in the case of vertical integration, due to difficulties in observing effort levels and service quality.

Development of a Make-or-Buy Decision-supporting Process | 51

Example: Many airlines belong to an alliance, wherein they benefit from high passenger demand as a result of alliance branding prestige. If an airline in this group offers a lesser service compared to other airlines, it can save on costs, but still benefit from alliance branding.

Solution: Imposing minimum quality, skill and advertising requirements, and controlling them frequently may reduce free-rider incentives, but is also very costly.

- **In05' Avoid "Buy-in" hazard**

Description: Buying-in refers to the practice (in the case of outsourcing) of attempting to obtain a contract award by offering a price less than anticipated costs with the expectation of: (1) increasing the contract price during the period of performance through, e.g., change orders or (2) receiving future follow-on contracts at prices high enough to recover any losses from the original buy-in contract (Defense Federal Acquisition Regulation Supplement, 2006).

Example: Minimum credible cost means that some cost items are neglected (Koelle, 2003). In particular, in the case of the space sector, these items include: premature loss charge cost, mission abort surcharge cost, certification cost, financing cost, product improvement cost, administration cost and fees. Unrealistic cost assumptions allow the supplier to offer an unfairly competitive contract.

Solution: If possible, the buyer should retain title of the specialized assets and loan them to his supplier. This is also called quasi-vertical integration. Opportunism by the supplier can then be countered by transferring assets to more cooperative suppliers (Monteverde & Teece, 1982a). Another possibility is that the buyer obtains, from the supplier, a binding price commitment ex-ante by employing multi-year procurements or price options for additional quantities (Defense Federal Acquisition Regulation Supplement, 2006).

- **In06' Reduce compensation-related incentive to lease**

Description: Compensation plans can create incentives to lease; e.g., a manager whose bonus depends on the return on invested capital will lease rather than purchase assets. If products "must" be produced in-house, this proposition has no impact, because managers do not have the option to lease.

52 Development of a Make-or-Buy Decision-supporting Process

Example: In the aerospace sector, this may happen for small products, such as leasing tools, but it may also happen for large activities, such as leasing a complete production plant.

Solution: A solution is to include the capitalized value of lease payments in invested capital calculations (Smith & Watts, 1982).

f) Vertical Integration Pros Submodule (Stability Aspects)

- **In07 Reduce risk concerning quality**

  Description: Contracting may be imperfect (i.e., imperfect contract) if some attributes of the input are not verifiable by third parties. For example, in some cases, the quality of an input can be observed by collaborating partners, but cannot be verified by a court of law. If a contract that stipulates a given price for an agreed quantity is signed, a supplier could lower its costs by reducing quality. The final goods producer would be obliged to buy the inferior products without recourse (Grossman & Helpman, 2002). Another disadvantage in this field is the difficulty for the buyer to monitor the complete production life-cycle from the supplier: while an employer has control rights over an employee, e.g., concerning the manner in which the work is performed, a buyer does not have those rights over an independent supplier. In this case, just the outcome of the work can be controlled (Masten, 1988).

  If maintaining the quality of a part is critical for the overall success of the final product, it is useful to produce the part in-house. Akerlof (1970) first noted the adverse selection problem (sometimes referred to as the lemon problem) that arises from the inability of buyers to differentiate between the quality of certain products. The most cited example is the used car industry, in which the seller operates at a comparative advantage as others in the market cannot tell if he is selling a "lemon" (i.e., poor quality car). Consequently, there is risk involved in purchasing these goods and, while at the product's low price, buyers are willing to take this risk and traders who sell quality cars are not willing to sell at such a low prices. This proposition is important to situations in which quality is critical for success.

  Example: Buying a poor quality car is relatively less fatal than buying a poor quality aircraft or rocket. Therefore, efforts to avoid adverse selection effects from the buyer and government are much more important for the aerospace sector than for any other sector.

Development of a Make-or-Buy Decision-supporting Process 53

Solution: This problem can be avoided if the buyer completes transactions with those suppliers that have established reputations for quality or from those that offer warranties for their products. The buyer should outsource first for less critical components and later on outsource for more critical ones after she has gained more experience with the potential supplier (Quinn & Hilmer, 1995). Quality uncertainty ex-ante can be reduced by licensing and/or certification practices (Akerlof, 1970). For example, certifications, such as a high school diploma or Ph.D., indicate the attainment of certain levels of proficiency.

- **In08 Increase reliability of receiving an input**
  Description: Companies sometimes face a short supply of particular inputs. Motivation for non-market procurement ensures the supply of important inputs.
  Example: In the aerospace industry, buyers have generally well-working, reliable supply channels, so this advantage is of minor interest. However, Boeing is an exception, as the company recently rescheduled the first test flight for its B787 as it wrestled with software problems and a shortage of bolts.

- **In09 Reduce poaching**
  Description: Poaching means the misuse of information or expertise that is given in trust for the accomplishment of a specific purpose, now used for the gain of the recipient of the information and to the detriment of the giver (Klein, Crawford & Al-chian, 1978). It is easier to control proprietary information when dealing with internal employees than with suppliers. However, outsourcing often requires providing suppliers with valuable knowledge-assets, e.g., the organization's production processes, which may then be leaked to competitors. In particular, this is a delicate problem when suppliers are dealing with several competing buyers.
  While exact imitations are hard to determine, leaking knowledge may lead to innovative substitution based on a combination of leaked knowledge of the giver and complementary knowledge of the recipient (Schumpeter, 1989). Malerba and Orsenigo (1995) distinguish between the Schumpeter I technological pattern and the Schumpeter II technological pattern: Schumpeter I technologies are short-lived and quick to be replaced by new technologies, resulting in minor imitation risk. Schumpeter II technologies are long-lived and new technologies complement them, or are based on them, resulting in high imitation risk. Companies should retain core com-

petencies within the organization, not only to prevent other companies from developing similar capabilities, but also to enhance the development of core competencies (Prahalad & Hamel, 1990).

Example: Each technology transferred to China's plants must be certified with a China Compulsory Certification (CCC). This certification reveals sensitive data that enables plagiarism (Shinde, 2007). Mitsubishi Heavy Industries learned how to operate a launcher from JAXA, which outsourced this activity to them. Other organizations now have an interest in subcontracting with Mitsubishi to benefit from its launcher operations expertise. In particular, in the space sector, organizations or countries are very sensitive as to whether proprietary information is available for competitors or to other nations, due to national security.

Solution: Schumpeter II technologies are typically one source of a company's competitive advantage. Thus, imitation risk might be reduced by only outsourcing activities related to Schumpeter I technologies and/or, by fragmenting Schumpeter II technologies know-how to several suppliers so that the information given to each of the recipients alone is useless.

- **In10 Increase foreclosure**

  Description: Foreclosure occurs when practices are adopted, such as vertical integration, that reduce competitive buyers' access to suppliers (i.e., upstream foreclosure) or competitive sellers' access to buyers (i.e., downstream foreclosure) (Hart et al., 1990).

  Example: In the aerospace industry, the probability of applying foreclosure is low, because competitor reactions will cause negative effects in the long run (e.g., the competitor will build up his own aluminum supply chain, which may compete with the foreclosed production plant) that outweigh the achieved benefits in the short run.

- **In11' Avoid high competitiveness costs**

  Description: Competitiveness costs are, among others, internal costs that result from poor and unstable supplier quality (Richardson, 1993). The time and effort necessary to manage partnerships (ex-post) is generated by this typical kind of transaction cost perpetrator.

Development of a Make-or-Buy Decision-supporting Process 55

Example: Typically, aerospace subsystems are tested from the final assembler before they are assembled, even though these subsystems have already been tested by the supplier.

Solution: Suppliers are required to comply with the Boeing Quality Management System, a blend of ISO 9001:2000 and aerospace quality standards. In doing so, Boeing inspectors do not need to inspect all parts before they are assembled. If Boeing can be assured that a supplier has a good internal process and maintains quality standards, then as long as the inspectors are able to watch the process, they do not have to spend so much time watching the parts. (Destefani, 2004)

- **In12' Avoid expensive contracts**

Description: Complete contracts are expensive because they must specify exactly what is expected of each party under all possible contingencies, and require negotiation and enforcement (Hart, 1995). Technological uncertainty, remote dates for contract performance and creativity are variables that increase the cost of drafting complete contracts (see: In13' Reduce hold-up problem). But even in those situations wherein all relevant variables can be clearly specified in a contract, the threat of production delays during litigation may be an effective bargaining device for the supplier (Klein, Crawford & Alchian, 1978). Any contract is therefore still subject to post-contractual opportunistic behavior. This results in a loss of efficiency. For example, the buyer may decide to hold standby facilities that are otherwise not worthwhile, as argued by Klein, Crawford and Alchian (1978). In this context, it should be noted that the use of concurrent sourcing (i.e., simultaneously making and buying the same good) can be used as a sanctioning device (Parmigiani, 2007) since it enables the buyer to more easily switch from outsourcing to vertical integration, if necessary.

Example: Boeing's approach is to slowly ramp up the amount of work given to a new supplier (Destefani, 2004). This can build trust over time.

Solution: Incomplete contracts can be used wherein details are omitted and left open for future renegotiation. However, future renegotiation motivates sub-optimal investment, because it leaves unclear, e.g., how gains from investments are distributed among the parties. For these and other reasons, the degree of the contract's incompleteness should be based on the trade-off between the costs of implementing more complete agreements and the benefits that arise from a reduction in opportunistic behaviors to redistribute the contractual surplus (Crocker & Reynolds, 1993).

The aimed degree of completeness/incompleteness is particularly important to selecting the appropriate contract type in determining compensation. The most complete type is the Firm-Fixed Price contract (FFP), wherein price is negotiated ex-ante. The most flexible type is the Fixed-Price Incentive Successive targets contract (FPIS), wherein nonbinding target prices are periodically negotiated ex-post (Federal Acquisition Regulation, 2005). As the complexity of a technological system increases, contracts are more incomplete and thereby pose greater contractual hazards (Grossman & Hart, 1986). Thus, vertical integration is more beneficial than vertical outsourcing. In this vein, Arrow (1969) calls attention to norms of social behavior. He observes that it is useful for individuals to trust each other's word, because in the absence of trust, it is very costly to arrange for sanctions, guarantees, etc., as described above.

- **In13' Reduce hold-up problem**

  <u>Description</u>: Hart (1995) shows that the absence of ex-ante contracts creates a potential hold-up problem. Production typically requires investment in assets. Firm-specific assets are those assets that are more valuable in their current use than in their next best alternative use (Klein, Crawford & Alchian, 1978). In this way, once a supplier specializes in its production for a particular final good, these inputs have no value to other companies – it is not possible to switch to another buyer without additional investment costs.

  This argument suggests that the likelihood of outsourcing decreases with the specificity of the asset. In addition, the likelihood of outsourcing decreases the more the environmental situation is uncertain, because it is impossible to specify what actions each party should perform under all possible future contingencies. Buyers can threaten to refuse delivery of components unless the supplier's price is lowered (i.e., hold-up between companies). Thus, the supplier is in a relatively weak bargaining position ex-post negotiation. Under such a threat, the supplier will rationally underinvest in specific assets (i.e., underinvestment) (Holmstrom, 1999).

  Overinvestment can also occur when influence activities are involved (Lafontaine & Slade, 2007). For example, if the government subsidizes a company, overinvestment is likely to occur. Buyers can also be in a weak bargaining position ex-post negotiation. High switching costs may lock the assembler into dependence upon a supplier and thereby expose that assembler to opportunistic re-contracting, or to the loss of transaction-specific expertise and skills (Monteverde & Teece, 1982b). If (accidentally) a key component has been outsourced, the buyer loses strategic flexibility, e.g., to introduce a new product when he wants, rather than when the supplier permits (Quinn & Hilmer, 1995). Even if a non-key component has been outsourced, the buyer may lose control over a supplier, e.g., when the buyer does not have enough market power relative to the seller. According to Ouchi (1981), the hazard of opportunism from suppliers is absent in the less integrated Japanese industry. This is caused, among other things, by the fact that the relationship between the final assembler and the supplier is one of whole cooperation in Japan.

Example: Once an airline decides to buy from Producer A, the airline also has an incentive to buy again from the same producer in order to maintain the family concept (same cockpits result in no additional costs for pilots to train, same subsystems result in inexpensive maintenance, etc.). Therefore, the producer also has a strong incentive to offer a complete family concept to the airline; even if one aircraft type's marginal costs for production are higher than the price quoted. In the case of the aerospace sector, buyers have few (if any) alternative suppliers ex-post, owing to the extensive lead-time and costs required for development and production of aerospace systems. As a consequence, buyers are in a weak bargaining position, because they cannot switch to an alternative supplier in the short-term.

Solution: Alternatives, besides vertical integration, are long-term supply contracts, exclusive selling rights, rights to veto expansion, etc. Contracts that specify bargaining power distribution between the partners can overcome the underinvestment problem. For example, giving all power to the investing party avoids underinvestment. However, this comes at the cost of writing or enforcing the contract. Another practiced option (similar to avoiding the "buy-in" hazard) is that the buyer owns key parts of the equipment. In this way, the seller needs to manufacture the goods for the buyer. If a conflict occurs, the buyer can simply remove his equipment, forcing the seller to stop production (Quinn & Hilmer, 1995). Increased bargaining power by creating contracts with more than one partner is a common alternative as well. Heide and John (1988) suggest that the supplier should make offsetting investments that create exit barriers for the buyer, e.g., create an identity in connection with the buyer's product ("Intel inside" stickers on laptop computers, for example), establish personal relationships with the buyer's employees (workshops, training groups, events) and add further value to the product (before-during-after service).

- **In14' Avoid first-mover advantage of supplier**

Description: The specifications of newly designed aerospace subsystems are often unknown ex-ante. Consequently, pre-production heuristic development generates supplier's production and design knowledge. Thus, a supplier working on pre-production development gains a first-mover advantage, because of the knowledge acquired during development (Monteverde & Teece, 1982b). In particular, when the company seeks technological or quality leadership positions, vertical integration is appropriate (Harrigan, 1984).

Example: About 35% of Boeing's 787 "Dreamliners'" major systems are produced in Japan. This can become a strategic threat to Boeing (i.e., the buyer), who globally outsources (e.g., to Japan), according to Goldstein's (2002) three-stage process for the developing domestic aviation sector. These three stages include: (1) the foreign country starts with co-production agreements; (2) a viable set of subcontractors develop in the foreign country; and (3) the foreign country's industry is capable of putting all subsystems together and becoming a final assembler of complete aircraft. Perhaps inexplicable is the fact that current US policy is framed with respect to national security issues, rather than economic concerns, regarding global outsourcing. For instance, contracts valued over $5 million (only) must be screened to ensure that sensitive technologies are not delivered to potentially hostile nations (Pritchard, 2001).

Solution: In contrast to Boeing, Airbus only subcontracts internationally for the subsystems of its older models, while subsystems for its newer models are produced in Europe (Smith, 2001; Pritchard, 2001). By doing so, one can assume that Airbus avoids the opportunity for foreign countries to develop state-of-the-art subcontractors that one day may gain competence to produce and assemble novel aircraft at lower costs than Airbus.

- **In15' Reduce cultural risk**

Description: Differences in regulatory traditions, customers and beliefs about management, economic development, political infrastructure and memberships in economic blocks may increase the riskiness of foreign expansion (Pennings, 1994).

Cultural risk related to confidentiality of critical information and loss of control is especially important when accounting functions are outsourced (Manabat, 2003). Thus, it can be assumed that domestic outsourcing is more likely to succeed than foreign outsourcing. However, Lafontaine and Slade (2007) discover that the prediction from basic agency theory, that increased risk makes integration more likely, is not supported by empirical studies. They explain this discrepancy with the fact that, in some situations, agents have more information about local market conditions.

Example: The costs, from manufacturing to management, in Japanese companies have already been estimated at the stage of planning and design. The price that a customer is willing to pay for a product is first estimated and serves as the basis for calculating prices of component parts, ranging from design to sales (Chen, 2004). In contrast, the typical method in the USA and Europe is to design first, and then estimate cost based on a series of standard costs, such as labor cost, materials cost and manufacturing cost. Each item is calculated and is then totaled by the accountant. If the cost is too high, design will be modified and calculated again. These different approaches may cause misunderstandings and delays in international cooperation.

Solution: Opening centers in multiple countries helps to minimize single location risks.

g) Vertical Integration Pros Submodule (Coordination Aspects)

- **In16 Improve price coordination**

Description: It may be optimal from a company-wide standpoint to set prices for products and services wherein some units sustain losses. Independent units care only about their own profits. However, if the company owns its units, it can coordinate prices and service costs. In particular, firms with reference to network industries require extensive coordination (Carlton & Klamer, 1983).

Example: In order to offer passengers proper transfer connections, airlines must operate short-distance flights (from spoke to hub and from hub to spoke) at a loss (i.e., seat load factor is low) to ensure that their long-distance flights (from hub to hub) are fully booked. Because long-distance flights have the potential for higher profits; the loss in short-distance flights is compensated by the profit gained from the airline's long-distance flights.

- **In17 Reduce taxes**

  Description: Assuming that profits at different stages of production are differently taxed, total taxes can be reduced by shifting profits to low-tax activities. One way to realize this is when low-tax units charge higher transfer prices to high-tax units. However, this type of activity is limited by tax authorities (Scholes et al., 2005). Further tax advantages arise from different treatments of gains and losses: tax is paid to the government when income is generated, but the government does not bill the company when losses occur. Therefore, based on analysis by Majd and Myers (1987), a vertically integrated company pays less in taxes than its businesses would pay separately.

  Example: In the case of aerospace organizations, tax reductions are a moderate advantage. The portfolio of large aerospace organizations, such as Boeing, EADS or Lockheed Martin, typically includes aircraft, launchers and satellites for both commercial and military purposes. As history shows, while a company's commercial aircraft division may be profitable, its military-launcher division may sustain losses, or vice versa.

- **In18' Avoid double marginalization**

  Description: Double marginalization occurs when there are successive stages of a non-integrated monopoly (Spengler, 1950). As a result, each monopolist applies margins to raise prices above marginal costs. In contrast, a vertically integrated monopolist applies only one margin (i.e., single marginalization).

  Example: There exist many monopolies and/or oligopolies in the aerospace sector. However due to the complexity of aerospace products, it is difficult to create a vertically integrated monopolist.

- **In19' Avoid high set-up costs**

  Description: It is costly to search for a suitable input supplier (while a specialized component producer must find a potential final goods producer), with costs incurred such as: bargaining costs, decision-costs and supplier development costs for training and technology transfer (Richardson, 1993). Time and effort are necessary to the manage partnerships (ex-ante) generated by this typical kind of transaction cost perpetrator.

Development of a Make-or-Buy Decision-supporting Process

Example: NASA sponsors tournaments to determine which supplier will obtain the contract for the development of a new launcher; coordination of these tournaments is very costly.

Solution: Increasing the contract period with suppliers reduces the frequency of search activities.

- **In20' Avoid difficulty to set incentives**

Description: A company must try to provide its partners with incentives to produce inputs to its specifications, and in the quantity that it demands. In the case of a joint venture, the challenge is to set incentives in such a way that the person who makes the final decision acts in the best interests of the joint venture as a whole, as opposed to any one of its individual members (Rowan, 2004).

Example: Airbus plans to assemble A320 jets in China under a 51%-owned joint venture with a consortium of local, state-owned companies. According to Airbus China President Laurence Barron, this treaty will strengthen Airbus' ties with the Chinese government. It will also make the relationship reciprocal by sharing aircraft-making knowledge. (Ng, 2007)

Solution: Long-term goals make contract negotiations easier, because the strategic pathway of two parties is more similar in the long run, than operational driven tactical decisions are in the short run.

- **In21' Avoid phantom limb pain**

Description: Lost interaction effects with outsourced activities (independently on their core or non-core status) can diminish the effectiveness of the remaining activities (Mahnke, 2001).

Example: Airlines outsource the handling of passenger luggage at airports. Even though airlines try to offer the best service for their first class passengers, passenger satisfaction can suffer as a result of dirty, damaged, delayed or lost luggage.

Solution: An organization can ensure that its remaining employees interact closely with its outsourced activities (Quinn & Hilmer, 1995). Alternately, the organization can handle "losses" better by finding and implementing alternatives, if the process of outsourcing is slower.

- **In22' Avoid high transportation cost**

  Description: By primarily outsourcing, the distance between the buyer and supplier is greater than if the activity is vertically integrated. This results in higher fuel consumption cost, higher airport or port fees, higher environmental penalties and longer reaction time for solving production troubles or supply shortfalls.

  Example: According to Airbus China President Laurence Barron, it might cost more to build the A320s in China than at its plants in Europe because of reduced aircraft part transportation costs from Europe and the longer industrial cycle in China (Ng, 2007).

  Solution: Motivating aerospace suppliers to reside in close proximity to the buyer's plants, as practiced by the automobile industry, in coherence with just-in-sequence philosophy is one solution that avoids high transportation cost. Toyota's factories in Japan and the USA are examples of large-scale integrators and suppliers that are located near one another.

h) Outsourcing Pros Submodule (Control Aspects)

- **Out01 Achieve high-powered incentives**

  Description: Holmstrom and Milgrom (1991) model the choice of organizational form in a setting in which an agent must perform multiple tasks for the principal. They show that "high-powered incentives" are more common when the agent owns the productive asset (outsourcing relationship), than when the principal owns the asset (employment relationship). According to Gibbons' (2005) explanation, all employee incentives come only from being paid on measured performance, while supplier incentives come from two sources: payments based on measured performance and the asset's value after production occurs. Thus, in a typical outsourcing relationship, it is the supplier who fronts the cost of the inputs necessary to manufacture components, unless the principal chooses to include a fixed payment for this purpose in the contract offer. If the project fails, the supplier stands to lose his investment. This means that a supplier has more at stake than a manager. Disadvantageously, under such a threat, the investing supplier will rationally under-invest (Grout, 1984) in the relationship (see: In13' Reduce hold-up problem).

  Example: The buyer must also indirectly incur some of the risk for the supplier that is incurred as a result of (too) expensive aerospace products.

Development of a Make-or-Buy Decision-supporting Process

- **Out02' Avoid bureaucratic distortions**

  Description: In the case of vertical integration, there are high costs of producing components, because the company has many divisions to manage. This causes high governance costs, due to attenuated incentives and bureaucratic distortions. Hayek (1945) argues that these costs arise from the fact that knowledge is dispersed among several people in the organization. McAfee and McMillan (1995) develop a model that relays this claim. They find that production costs increase in the length of a company's hierarchical structure. Generally, people in organizations devote energy to influencing the organization's decisions to their advantage (Milgrom, 1988). More specifically, a cost of communication exists, because people have incentive to exploit their informational advantages. This effect increases cumulatively as the information moves up the hierarchy. Therefore, longer hierarchies have greater informational inefficiencies: "The larger any organization becomes, the weaker is the control over its actions exercised by those at the top" (Downs, 1966, p. 109), resulting in diminishing returns-to-scale (i.e., Law of Diminishing Control).

  According to Williamson (1967), a manager trades off wideness for depth in undertaking any expansion of his resource units. He has more resources under his control, but the quality (serial reproduction loss) and the quantity (bounded capacity constraint) of his information is lowered and can be even more reduced if goals differ between hierarchical levels. Williamson's (1967) model shows that the optimal number of hierarchical levels is between 4 and 7, assuming that the span of control is in normal ranges and that the organization employs between 1000 and 100 000 employees.

  Example: The aerospace industry is strongly affected by this argument because of its historical origin, wherein aerospace organizations are strongly driven by a high-performance-whatever-it-costs philosophy, rather than optimal organizational behavior. Aerospace companies are also typically very large, internationally oriented and influenced by many stakeholders, so that it is very difficult to communicate a clear "order."

  Solution: Much of the information that top management needs for planning must come from below in the organizational hierarchy. A Japanese company's ability to utilize production information from the lowest level of organization is one of the sources of the country's competitiveness, according to Aoki (1988). Levine and Tyson (1990) find that employee participation in decision-making improves company's productivity, because the information that workers have, and managers lack, about the workplace can be used. Downs (1966) names the following countermeasures for controlling loss: external data checks, redundancy, creation of overlapping areas of responsibility, and reorganization to keep the hierarchy flat.

- **Out03' Avoid costly incentives for motivating efficient production**
Description: Companies must adopt costly incentives and control systems to motivate internal managers to engage in efficient production, otherwise, free-rider effects will occur within vertical integration. There is a misalignment of incentives between central and internal managers.
Example: In the aerospace industry, every task must be recorded to meet strict aircraft licensing rules. Based on this, the free-rider effect is nearly prevented, thus, this argument is of minor interest.
Solution: An attempt may be made to invest in the company culture, such as enhanced good will, teamwork and ethical understandings to address this concern.

i) Outsourcing Pros Submodule (Stability Aspects)

- **Out04 Achieve spreading of risk**
Description: Risk, while impossible to eliminate, can be diversified and spread throughout a corporation. Burgers, Hill and Chan Kim (1993) argue that demand uncertainty motivates competitors to enter into strategic alliances in order to gain access to the capabilities required to cope with such uncertainty. Burgers et al. (1993) imply that poorly performing companies are more likely have an incentive to enter into alliances than efficiently operating enterprises. The reason for this is that poorly performing companies are likely less able to deal with the adverse consequences of uncertainties and/or persistent competitive battles.
Example: One source for funding the A380 development comes from risk-sharing partners other than Airbus partners and their national governments' funding, according to Esty (2004). These risk-sharing partners agreed to bear a certain amount of the development costs, which would be repaid on a per plane basis, in exchange for the right to become exclusive suppliers for the A380 (Esty, 2004). Unfavorably for Airbus, might be the commitment to accept the risk-sharing partners as exclusive suppliers, because exclusive suppliers might have the incentive to benefit from this dependency (increase prices, decrease quality, etc.) at the expense of Airbus. Over-

Development of a Make-or-Buy Decision-supporting Process

all, the advantages of a low-risk funding program are assumed to outweigh the disadvantages of dependency.

- **Out05 Avoid high cost of ownership transfer**

  Description: When the useful life of a general (i.e., non-company specific) asset is significantly longer than the period over which a company expects to use the asset and when the costs of ownership transfer are high, it may be advantageous to lease, rather than buy, the asset (Smith & Wakeman, 1985). In particular, leasing reduces the costs for information on quality compared to purchasing (Flath, 1980).

  Example: An airline that leases an aircraft is less concerned about its condition than an airline that plans to buy the aircraft.

- **Out06 Deter market entry**

  Description: Setting up partnerships with potential competitor can deter their market entry.

  Example: An incumbent airline may offer a potential entrant airline to share expensive facilities, not for the purpose of economies of scale, but to discourage the entrant from building its own facility and entering the market at a more competitive scale (Chen & Ross, 2000).

- **Out07 Achieve stable set of clients**

  Description: Random variation in demand for services from any one client can be compensated for by a larger set of clients (Clemons & Hitt, 1997).

  Example: An aerospace organization typically has a high incentive to produce, not only for its country of origin, but also to export its products.

- **Out08 Achieve high program flexibility**

  Description: The buyer can convert the fixed cost of payroll to a variable cost using temporary staffing. Thus, the buyer can expand or shrink programs in a short period versus maintaining company employees. In this scenario, downsizing is possible without the disadvantageous publicity entailed by layoffs (Bean, 2003).

  Example: Temporary staffing is typical in the aerospace industry because the development phase for new aircraft, rockets, etc., requires substantial labor, while the period thereafter requires only moderate resources for product improvements, maintenance, etc. In addition, passenger demand is cyclical, resulting in the fact that airlines lease an average of one-third (Heinemann, 2007) of their fleet to adjust to changing market conditions. Currently, General Electric Commercial Aviation Services (GECAS) and the International Lease Finance Corporation (ILFC) dominate the aircraft leasing service market.

- **Out09 Increase sharing of R&D costs**
Description: New product innovations are often high-cost activities and the required assets are beyond the capabilities of a single company. Thus, horizontal or vertical cooperation may be the only viable means for improvement (Teece, 1992). In addition, collaborative R&D reduces needless duplication of efforts, i.e., avoidance of near-identical technological paths (David, 1985).
Example: Development of the International Space Station (ISS) may not be feasible for one country alone, from a financial and resource point of view.

j) Outsourcing Pros Submodule (Coordination Aspects)

- **Out10 Increase sales**
Description: According to Frynas, Mellahi and Pigman (2006), global outsourcing has the advantage of collaboration and consultation with foreign industry and foreign policymakers. Consequently, one of the goals of outsourcing is to secure a sale that would not take place in the absence of compensatory provisions. In the literature (Wessner, 1999), this is called industrial offset. Direct offsets involve production sharing, technology transfer or worker training, whereas indirect offsets can include counter trades. Industrial offsets are common in the aerospace market, where unit-selling prices are high and buyers are strictly regulated by governments.
Example: In 1974, Boeing contracted with Mitsubishi in Japan to produce flaps for the B747, which resulted in major sales of B747s to Japan (MacPherson & Pritchard, 2002).

- **Out11 Reduce labor costs**
Description: One of the basic incentives for outsourcing is to produce in regions where labor costs are lower than the home region. There is also a trend toward outsourcing work to more low-cost service industries, such as those located primarily in India. However, outsourcing in China, Thailand, Philippines, Russia, Bulgaria and Jamaica is also on the rise.

Development of a Make-or-Buy Decision-supporting Process 67

Example: Labor costs are typically at least 50% lower in the Asia-Pacific region than in Europe or the USA (MacPherson & Pritchard, 2002). According to the literature, it is estimated that 3,3 million white-collar jobs (equivalent to $136 billion in wages) will shift from the USA to low-cost countries by 2015 (Engardio, Bernstein & Kripalani, 2003).

- **Out12 Reduce careless activities**

  Description: Outsourcing is initiated to transform or reduce sloppy activities (Rebitzer & Taylor, 1991). However, according to Mahnke (2001), when employees fear losing their jobs through outsourcing, they are strongly reluctant to share their knowledge with external vendors.

  Example: This argument is of less relevance for the aerospace sector, because outsourcing is becoming the norm.

- **Out 13 Increase concentration on core competencies**

  Description: Concentration on core competencies means focusing owned resources on a set of core competencies, where the company sees a critical strategic need and where it has special capabilities of providing unique value to customers (Quinn, Doorley & Paquette, 1990). Quinn and Hilmer (1995) define core competency as follows. (1) Sets of skills and knowledge, such as product design, technology creation or customer service, rather than traditional function, such as engineering, production or sales. (2) Flexible long-term architectures that allow improving skills in areas that customers will continue to value over time. (3) A limited number of skill sets, typically less than three, because for a higher number of skill sets, a company might be unable to match the performance of its more focused competitors. (4) Areas where the company is able to dominate by performing skills more effectively than the competition. (5) Sets of skills that are captured within the company's system, rather than based on individuals whose dismissal might destroy company successes.

  Example: In order to increase the product palette, aerospace organizations are forced to reduce the depth of their production.

- **Out14 Reduce levels of management coordination**

  Description: Management can focus more on the company's core business, because the time spent managing peripheral activities is reduced as a result of outsourcing

(Quinn & Hilmer, 1995). Thus, fewer levels of management coordination are required, which results in lower transaction costs than are incurred in a more diversified organization.

Example: JAXA recently outsourced its launch operation division to Mitsubishi Heavy Industries in order to be more competitive in the international market for commercial launchers.

- **Out15' Avoid reduced initiative to invest**

  Description: One insight from property-rights theory is that a division's incentive to invest is reduced by the fear of hold-up from its parent company, e.g., extracting rents in the case of vertical integration (i.e., hold-up within a company). Unfortunately, stopping one hold-up problem using a formal instrument typically creates another hold-up problem (Gibbons, 2005).

  Example: This advantage is of minor interest to the aerospace sector because the parent company's interests should not exploit its divisions, which would result in a weak competitive position.

  Solution: An attempt to increase the incentive to invest may occur by repetition, to show that the investment is of beneficial value.

- **Out16' Avoid negative Net Present Value projects**

  Description: Jensen (1986) predicts that a vertically integrated company invests more in negative Net Present Value (NPV) projects than its divisions would if operated separately. This can be explained by the fact that different lines of business have access to more free cash flow as part of a vertically integrated company, than they otherwise would on their own.

  Example: This argument is of major interest to the aerospace sector because budgets are often allocated to fascinating projects rather than to economically feasible projects.

  Solution: An attempt to reduce investments in economically unfeasible projects may occur by establishing a committee to evaluate, e.g., the NPV of each project.

- **Out17 Reduce production costs**

  Description: Over time, suppliers adopt technological advances that lower production cost without lowering quality.

Development of a Make-or-Buy Decision-supporting Process 69

Example: This argument is of high importance to the aerospace sector because there is high incentive for aerospace suppliers to invest in niche products in order to become a pioneer in the industry as well as to produce at a low cost, so that other companies have less interest in entering the market.

- **Out18' Avoid insufficient volume**
Description: It is typically difficult to generate sufficient volume to capitalize on returns-to-scale effects in production. Returns-to-scale is the relationship between output and a proportional variation of all inputs, taken together. Firms can produce the optimal volume and sell the surplus in the open market. Thus, this choice requires firms to enter a new market, which is not its primary line of business. An empirical study conducted by Berger and Ofek (1995) suggests that diversified organizations often perform poorly relative to those that are more focus oriented.
Example: The typical (aerospace) company has increasing returns-to-scale when output is low, followed by constant returns-to-scale as output increases, and decreasing returns-to-scale when output is high, as demonstrated by Berndt, Friedlaender and Wang Chiang (1990).
Solution: However, the proposition to avoid insufficient volume does not hold for all types of customers that the company wishes to target. Customers with higher incomes demand more differentiation or even customized and less standardized products. Small companies can satisfy these demands better than large ones. These small companies typically produce only a very small volume of products.

- **Out19 Achieve bundling of knowledge**
Description: Bundling knowledge at one physical place enables efficient use by participants (Clemons & Hitt, 1997).
Example: Airlines enjoy advantages over alternative forms of single-briefing offices before each flight.

- **Out20 Achieve expanding resources**
Description: Outsourcing can achieve an expansion of resources such that it reduces a company's development phase – assuming its manpower resource is constant – as multiple suppliers work simultaneously on individual components of a system that are on the critical path (Quinn & Hilmer, 1995).

70 Development of a Make-or-Buy Decision-supporting Process

Example: Without immense use of suppliers as resources, NASA would not have been able to develop the Saturn V rocket within one decade.

- **Out21 Gain access to benefits of partner's assets**

Description: A contractor with little experience in the country where the project is located, but with specialized skills, should team up with one who has an established organization, political or other valuable relationship in the country (Rowan, 2004). By doing so, the contractor gains access to new technologies, resulting in improved performance, new product innovation (Rothaermel, Hitt & Jobe, 2006) and customers, resulting in growth in market power. Diversification of new business is applicable in the case of strategic alliances.

Example: An alliance with Airline B enables Airline A to obtain access to valuable rare slots at airports that were originally designated for Airline B. The structure of labor markets in Japan, in particular, wherein lifetime employment is commonly practiced, leads to a relatively homogeneous and slowly adjustable labor force mixture, which is disadvantageous to satisfying fast-changing market trends. Therefore, Japanese companies are encouraged to utilize suppliers as efficient sources of disparate labor inputs (Smitka, 1991). This is one reason why Japanese aerospace companies are less vertically integrated compared to Western companies.

- **Out22 Develop technical standards**

Description: Competitors benefit from partial cooperation in reference to defining standards. This is applicable, in particular, in the case of strategic alliances or other forms of hierarchical, same-level corporations.

Example: Partners agree to only use a specific plug for their aircraft modules to allow easy replacement of certain modules built by different companies.

- **Out23' Avoid little learning effects**

Description: Vertical integration leads to a high cost of producing components because the firm does not benefit from learning that comes with specializing in a single activity (Grossman & Helpman, 2002). Specialization greatly enhances the standard of living of a society. However, companies benefit from economies of scope, because skills and resources can be used in related markets. According to Nayyar (1993), benefits from economies of scope are available for related, but not for unrelated, diversifications. Benefits from economies of scope for related products are

Development of a Make-or-Buy Decision-supporting Process 71

partly reduced by the negative effect on demand because of the capability to substitute a product when the price of another increases.

Example: In the long-range wide-body market segment, introduction of Airbus' A380 has a significantly negative effect on the price and sales of Boeing's B747, but an even greater adverse affect on the Airbus' A330 and A340 (Irwin & Pavcnik, 2004). However, Airbus' overall market share is assumed to increase because synergies that exist in owning all Airbus family planes might induce airlines to switch from Boeing planes to Airbus planes. This result highlights the fact that as companies expand their product line over time, profit maximization becomes more complicated as demand for a particular company's existing models is sensitive to the price and characteristics of its new models.

Solution: Companies must either specialize in one activity or produce related products to benefit from learning effects.

- **Out24 Attract higher-quality specialists**

  Description: Suppliers are able to attract higher-quality specialists because its operational scale provides future career opportunities for more specialized positions, than a less focused company can provide.

  Example: This argument is of less importance to the aerospace sector because buyers also offer many specialized positions.

- **Out25 Achieve availability of better specialists**

  Description: External specialists are likely to be better specialists (Domberger, 1998). However, Mahnke (2001) argues that if an activity has been poorly managed internally, due to lack of specialist knowledge, it is questionable that those managers are any better at communicating their needs to external providers.

  Example: This argument, to achieve availability of better specialists, is one of the typical incentives for aerospace organizations to hire specialized consultants. However, Mahnke has many doubts on the efficiency of this choice, which should be acknowledged.

k) Results Submodule

- **Res01 Sub-benefit of each setting item**

  Description: This item shows the vertical integration and outsourcing sub-benefits of each setting item. This result helps to identify those setting items that are strongly influenced by either vertical integration or outsourcing.

- **Res02 Sub-benefit of each adjusted setting item**

  Description: This item shows the vertical integration and outsourcing sub-benefits of each adjusted setting item. This result includes, in addition to Res01, influence from: strategic objectives, quasi-independent factors, and weighting of strategic objectives as well as quasi-independent factors.

- **Res03 Make-or-Buy ratio**

  Description: This item shows the total benefit of vertical integration and outsourcing as a fraction. All efforts have been taken to keep the graph simple.

--------------- *Description of items and propositions from page 46 to here* ---------------

4.2.3 Quantitative Assessment

a) Pre-assessment

For pre-assessment of approximately 50 propositions concerning outsourcing and vertical integration decisions two indicators are used, namely "potential" and "probability." The assessment of potential (What is the maximum positive, relative effect in terms of short-term profit, market share, etc., to the organization, when this circumstance occurs?) is measured on a five-point Likert-type (Babbie, 2000; Trochim, 2006) scale (+, ++, +++, ++++, +++++) wherein "+" represents a very poor proposition and "+++++" represents a very promising one. The assessment of the probability (How often does this circumstance occur?) is based on a five-point scale wherein "+" represents a proposition that very seldom occurs, and "+++++" represents a proposition that occurs very often. This pre-assessment method of propositions based on potential and probability, in general, is sufficiently reliable to preliminarily rank propositions. This ranking is helpful for accurate assessment, i.e., to spend relatively more time on significant propositions than on those ones with low potential and low probability.

Development of a Make-or-Buy Decision-supporting Process

Table 9: Vertical Integration Propositions

	Serial No.	Name	Potential	Probabil.	Signific.	Ranking
Control Aspects	In01	Achieve easy monitoring of employee's effort	++	+++++	++	7
	In02	Improve motivation by ownership effect	+	++++	+	16
	In03'	Avoid high trading costs	+++	+++++	+++	5
	In04'	Reduce free-rider problem	++++	+++	++	6
	In05'	Avoid "Buy-in" hazard	++	+	+	21
	In06'	Reduce compensation-related incentive to lease	+	+	+	22
Stability Aspects	In07	Reduce risk concerning quality	++++	++++	+++	3
	In08	Increase reliability of receiving an input	++	+++	+	11
	In09	Reduce poaching	++++	++	++	10
	In10	Increase foreclosure	+++	++	+	12
	In11'	Avoid high competitiveness costs	+++++	++	++	8
	In12'	Avoid expensive contracts	+++++	+++++	+++++	1
	In13'	Reduce hold-up problem	++++	++++	+++	4
	In14'	Avoid first-mover advantage of supplier	+++	+	+	20
	In15'	Reduce culture risk	+++	++	+	13
Coordination Aspects	In16	Improve price coordination	++++	+++++	++++	2
	In17	Reduce taxes	++	++	+	17
	In18'	Avoid double marginalization	+++	+++	++	9
	In19'	Avoid high set-up costs	+	++++	+	18
	In20'	Avoid difficulty to set incentives	++	++	+	19
	In21'	Avoid phantom limb pain	+++	++	+	14
	In22'	Avoid high transportation cost	++	+++	+	15

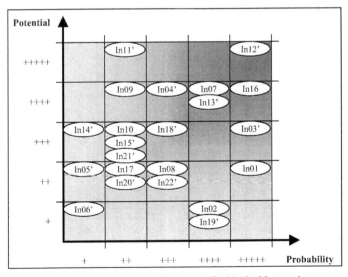

Figure 13: Potential-probability Matrix for Vertical Integration

74 Development of a Make-or-Buy Decision-supporting Process

Table 10: Outsourcing Propositions

	Serial No.	Name	Potential	Probabil.	Signific.	Ranking
Control	Out01	Achieve high-powered incentives	+++	+++	++	11
	Out02'	Avoid bureaucratic distortions	+++++	++++	++++	1
	Out03'	Avoid costly incentives for motivating effic. pod.	++	+	+	21
Stability Aspects	Out04	Achieve spreading of risk	+++	+++++	+++	6
	Out05	Avoid high cost of ownership transfer	+++	++	+	16
	Out06	Deter market entry	+++	+	+	20
	Out07	Achieve stable set of clients	++	++++	++	13
	Out08	Achieve high program flexibility	++++	+++++	++++	2
	Out09	Increase sharing of R&D costs	++	+++++	++	10
Coordination Aspects	Out10	Increase sales	+++	+++	++	12
	Out11	Reduce labor costs	+++++	++++	++++	3
	Out12	Reduce careless activities	+	+	+	23
	Out13	Increase concentration on core competencies	++++	++++	+++	5
	Out14	Reduce levels of management coordination	++++	+++	++	7
	Out15'	Avoid reduced initiative to invest	+	+	+	24
	Out16'	Avoid negative Net Present Value projects	++++	++	++	14
	Out17	Reduce production costs	+++++	++++	++++	4
	Out18'	Avoid insufficient volume	++++	+++	++	8
	Out19	Increase bundling of knowledge	++	++	+	19
	Out20	Achieve expanding resources	+++	++++	++	9
	Out21	Gain access to benefits of partner's assets	++++	++	++	15
	Out22	Develop technical standards	++	+	+	22
	Out23'	Avoid little learning effects	+++	++	+	17
	Out24	Attract higher-quality specialists	+	+	+	25
	Out25	Achieve availability of better specialists	+++	++	+	18

Table 9 and Table 10 show pre-assessment results for vertical integration and outsourcing. The "significance" is generated by multiplying the "potential" by the "probability" for each proposition. For better illustration, the symbol "+" is used instead of numbers, but calculation is based on numbers that are rounded-off. A more complex algorithm to calculate significance could be used, but would not improve the final process. Therefore, I concentrate on the procedure for developing this process, not on the mathematics. Figure 13 and Figure 14 show the related potential-probability matrix for vertical integration and outsourcing. Propositions that are in the significant sector (marked in dark gray) of these matrices require special attention because they influence the make-or-buy decision more than the others.

Development of a Make-or-Buy Decision-supporting Process

The philosophy of the potential-probability matrix is similar to the risk matrix. While the risk matrix is an effective tool used to guide the user to avoiding risks of high probability and high consequence (Alexander & Marshall, 2006), the potential-probability matrix illustrates the benefits of high potential and high probability.

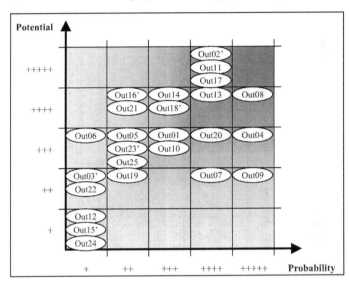

Figure 14: Potential-probability Matrix for Outsourcing

b) Detailed Assessment

For detailed assessment, a pairwise comparison (see Grob, 1984) is used to support the subjective-based assessment. This is a first approach method given uncertainty in a situation, where detailed studies are not yet been performed. The pairwise comparison method is a powerful tool that allows the researcher to perform a fair and comprehensive transparent ranking of criteria; it allows ranking and assessment of the relative weight of each proposition to be determined. However, results of pairwise comparisons must be checked for plausibility. Therefore, the relative benefit on each item of the "Settings" submodule that is gained from the propositions of the "Integration Pros" and "Outsourcing Pros" submodules are adjusted.

All results for vertical integration are incorporated in the input mask of the "Integration Pros" submodule, as shown in Table 11. Results for outsourcing are incorporated in the input mask of the "Outsourcing Pros" submodule, as shown in Table 12.

Table 11: Integration Pros Submodule

Serial No.		Strategic Objectives						Organization Character.			Product Character.				Environm. Character.			Sum
		Set01 Increase market share	Set02 Increase quality	Set03 Increase stability	Set04 Increase short-tem profit	Set05 Increase flexibility	Set06 Increase control	Set07 Organization size (high)	Set08 Technical experience (low)	Set09 Organizational skills (low)	Set10 Product complexity (high)	Set11 Asset specificity (high)	Set12 Strategic vulnerability (high)	Set13 Technology uncertainty (high)	Set14 Intensity of competition (high)	Set15 Market demand uncertainty (high)	Set16 Quality of business climate (low)	
Control Aspects	In01	0	8	2	2	0	8	8	0	0	5	0	8	2	0	0	8	51
	In02	5	5	5	8	0	0	0	0	0	0	0	2	0	0	0	0	25
	In03'	0	2	0	8	5	0	0	0	0	0	8	0	0	0	8	8	39
	In04'	0	8	2	8	0	2	8	0	0	0	0	5	0	0	0	0	33
	In05'	0	0	5	5	8	8	0	0	0	2	8	8	8	0	2	0	54
	In06'	0	0	0	5	2	5	0	0	0	0	0	0	0	0	0	0	12
Stability Aspects	In07	0	8	8	2	0	0	0	0	0	8	0	8	0	0	0	8	42
	In08	0	0	8	0	8	2	0	0	0	5	8	8	0	0	0	8	47
	In09	5	0	8	2	0	2	0	0	0	0	8	8	2	5	0	8	48
	In10	8	0	8	5	5	8	8	0	0	0	2	8	0	8	2	0	62
	In11'	0	0	0	2	8	0	0	0	0	0	2	2	5	0	0	5	24
	In12'	0	5	8	5	5	8	0	0	0	2	8	8	5	0	8	8	70
	In13'	0	5	8	5	8	5	0	0	0	5	8	8	0	0	0	5	57
	In14'	5	0	8	5	5	8	0	0	0	0	0	8	5	8	0	8	60
	In15'	0	0	5	0	0	8	2	0	0	2	5	8	2	0	0	8	40
Coordination Aspects	In16	2	0	2	8	2	5	8	0	0	0	0	5	0	5	8	0	45
	In17	0	0	0	5	0	0	8	0	0	0	0	0	0	0	0	0	13
	In18'	0	0	0	5	0	0	5	0	0	5	2	0	0	2	0	0	19
	In19'	0	0	0	5	2	2	0	0	0	2	5	5	8	0	5	8	42
	In20'	0	2	0	5	0	5	0	0	0	2	0	0	0	0	0	0	14
	In21'	0	0	2	5	0	0	0	0	0	5	5	5	0	0	0	0	22
	In22'	0	0	0	5	2	0	8	0	0	5	2	0	0	0	0	0	22
Sum		25	43	79	100	60	76	55	0	0	48	71	104	37	28	33	82	841

Note: Benefit that proposition "Inxx" has on item "Setyy"?

Scale: 0 = no effect; 1-3 = low effect; 4-6 = medium effect; 7-9 = high effect; 10 = 100% effect

Development of a Make-or-Buy Decision-supporting Process

Table 12: Outsourcing Pros Submodule

Serial No.		Strategic Objectives						Organization Character.			Product Character.				Environm. Character.			Sum
		Set01 Increase market share	Set02 Increase quality	Set03 Increase stability	Set04 Increase short-term profit	Set05 Increase flexibility	Set06 Increase control	Set07 Organization size (high)	Set08 Technical experience (low)	Set09 Organizational skills (low)	Set10 Product complexity (high)	Set11 Asset specificity (high)	Set12 Strategic vulnerability (high)	Set13 Technology uncertainty (high)	Set14 Intensity of competition (high)	Set15 Market demand uncertainty (high)	Set16 Quality of business climate (low)	
Control	Out01	0	0	0	5	0	0	0	0	0	0	0	2	0	0	0	2	9
	Out02'	0	2	2	8	5	2	8	0	8	5	0	0	0	0	0	2	42
	Out03'	0	2	0	8	0	5	5	0	2	0	0	0	0	0	0	0	22
Stability Aspects	Out04	0	0	8	2	2	0	0	0	0	8	5	8	8	0	8	8	57
	Out05	2	2	2	8	8	0	0	0	0	0	2	0	0	0	8	0	32
	Out06	5	0	6	4	0	5	0	0	0	0	5	8	0	8	2	0	43
	Out07	2	0	5	5	5	0	0	0	0	0	8	5	0	0	8	5	43
	Out08	2	0	5	5	8	0	0	0	0	2	0	0	5	0	8	5	40
	Out09	0	0	8	5	2	0	0	5	0	8	8	0	5	0	5	0	46
Coordination Aspects	Out10	7	0	3	7	0	0	0	0	0	0	0	7	0	8	2	2	36
	Out11	0	0	0	10	3	0	7	0	0	0	0	0	0	5	0	0	25
	Out12	0	5	2	7	3	7	9	0	0	0	0	0	0	2	0	3	38
	Out13	6	3	5	6	3	2	7	0	0	7	3	10	5	8	0	0	65
	Out14	0	3	5	5	8	5	8	0	5	5	0	8	0	0	0	0	52
	Out15'	8	0	5	5	0	0	0	0	0	0	8	5	0	0	0	0	31
	Out16'	0	0	0	4	0	2	6	0	0	5	0	0	5	0	6	0	28
	Out17	8	0	0	8	0	0	0	0	0	0	0	0	0	0	0	0	16
	Out18'	4	0	2	5	2	0	6	0	0	0	2	0	0	2	0	0	23
	Out19	0	5	5	5	5	0	0	0	0	0	0	0	0	0	2	0	22
	Out20	6	0	3	7	3	0	0	0	0	0	0	7	8	8	4	5	51
	Out21	8	0	3	4	0	0	0	0	0	2	5	6	3	5	3	0	39
	Out22	0	7	3	2	0	5	0	0	0	2	4	0	6	2	0	3	34
	Out23'	4	7	2	6	0	0	0	0	0	0	4	2	0	5	0	0	30
	Out24	0	3	2	4	0	0	0	0	0	0	5	5	0	0	0	0	19
	Out25	0	3	2	4	2	0	0	0	0	0	5	5	5	0	0	0	26
Sum		62	42	78	139	59	33	56	5	15	44	64	78	50	53	56	35	869

Note: Benefit that proposition "Outxx" has on item "Setyy"?

Scale: 0 = no effect; 1-3 = low effect; 4-6 = medium effect; 7-9 = high effect; 10 = 100% effect

Figure 15 illustrates the sub-benefits that vertical integration and outsourcing promise to each setting item. As can be seen, many setting items significantly benefit if activities are vertically integrated. These include: "Set06 Increase control," "Set12 Strategic vulnerability (high)" and "Set16 Quality of business climate (low)." The following setting items significantly benefit if activities are outsourced: "Set01 Increase market share," "Set04 Increase short-term profit," "Set14 Intensity of competition (high)" and "Set15 Market demand uncertainty (high)."

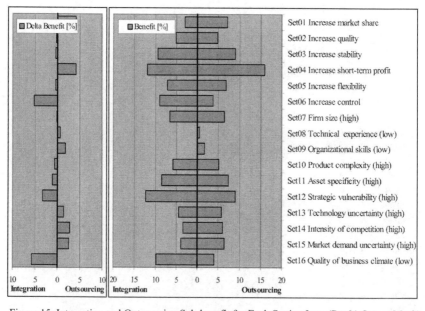

Figure 15: Integration and Outsourcing Sub-benefit for Each Setting Item (Res01 Output Mask)

4.3 Application of Process

4.3.1 General

To verify and use this process, the following four case studies are applied: (A) Copy machine usage (as a reference); (B) Aircraft final assembly production; (C) Satellite rocket launch operation; and (D) Space tourism rocket development. In the following, each case study is briefly introduced and then applied to the process.

Development of a Make-or-Buy Decision-supporting Process 79

4.3.2 Case Studies

For all cases, I examine the make-or-buy decision from the buyer's point of view. The buyer is typically a large aerospace organization that aims to implement its activities efficiently by determining the appropriate level of outsourcing/integration. Each case is assessed separately.

- **(A) Copy machine usage (as a reference):** The target is to copy office letters. On average, about ten office workers share a copy machine. Those copy machines are multi-use machines, meaning they are also used for printing, faxing and scanning documents. If one machine is out of order, it is easy to use another machine in a nearby location until the original is fixed. Currently, a large supply market for copy machines is available in any size, color, quality, etc. This case is the reference. History has shown that copy machines are typically leased to companies. Copy machines are produced by specialized organizations. Therefore, it would be very surprising for an aerospace company to develop and build its own copy machine just to copy daily office documents.

- **(B) Aircraft final assembly production:** The target is the final assembly of the aircraft, which means assembly of subsystems, such as wings, stabilizers, engines, fuselage, cabin interiors, etc., all for one main system – the aircraft. Today, only a few competitors have the expertise to assemble final aircraft. In the future, emerging competitors will arise. Short lead-times, low costs and high quality are key requirements for a successful final assembly line.

- **(C) Satellite rocket launch operation:** Note that this case is already discussed in Chapter 3. Here, I apply the process, rather than isolated theories, to the case. The target is to operate commercial rockets to satisfy nationally-owned satellite launches as well as providing overcapacity for the global satellite market. Competition between rocket operators is high. Low prices, high flexibility, complete customer services and high success rates are the key points used to gain new customers and maintain existing ones. The launcher that is currently used, an HII-A rocket, is based on proven technology. However, operating costs need to be reduced in order to remain competitive.

- **(D) Space tourism rocket development:** The target is to develop a small suborbital rocket with a capacity of up to five passengers. This rocket should be semi-reusable and permit weekly flights. Each flight should initially be sold for $200 000 (in 2008 dollars). The rocket should be in operation in 2015. Demand for such a flight is uncertain, as space tourism is a new market domain, and only market surveys are yet available to determine demand. Technology is available as shown by the successful test flights of Scaled Composite SpaceShipOne in 2004, but the certification process for passenger flights is a challenge with regard to safety and environmental concerns. Market competition is relatively low because only Scaled Composites has the proven necessary expertise to realize development of a suborbital rocket.

4.3.3 Results

With the case studies in mind, I apply the make-or-buy decision-supporting process in the following five phases, as shown in Figure 16. For this, I develop a tool entitled "MoB-Tool," as shown in Figure 17.

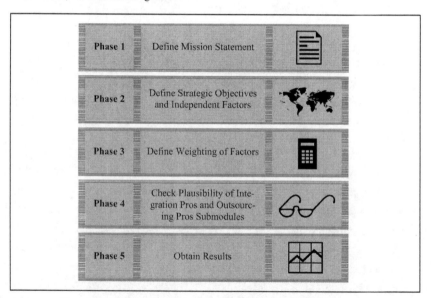

Figure 16: Application of the Make-or-Buy Decision-supporting Process

M₀B -Tool

A Make-or-Buy Decision-supporting Process by Robert A. Goehlich
Version 1.0

Instruction

yellow	= cell value must be determined
orange	= cell value can be changed
red	= cell shows results
Help	= provides information how to use
Data	= input is required by user
Fig.	= a graph is shown here
Scale	= defines range of operation

Comprehensive decision-support (1 week): use phase... | 1 | 2 | 3 | 4 | 5 |

Quick decision-support (1 hour): use phase... | | 2 | 3 | | 5 |

Validate and/or adjust tool (tbd): use phase... | | | | 4 | 5 |

Phase 1: Define Mission Statement

Help: Before defining the organization's strategic objectives, it is necessary to clearly define a mission statement.

Data: *"Provide society with superior aerospace products that improve the quality of life, satisfy customer needs, and provide employees with advancement opportunities and investors with a superior rate of return."*

Phase 1a: Define Activities

Help: Name the activities that should be investigated. Up to five activities can simultaneously be modeled.

Data:
Name of Activity 1 — (A) Copy machine usage (as reference)
Name of Activity 2 — (B) Aircraft final assembly production
Name of Activity 3 — (C) Satellite rocket launch operation
Name of Activity 4 — (D) Space tourism rocket development
Name of Activity 5 — Test integration

Phase 2: Define Strategic Objectives and Independent Factors (SETTINGS Submodule)

Help: The strategic objectives using the mission statement as a guide (profitability, market share, quality, cost, flexibility, dependability, innovation, etc.) need be defined for each case study. In addition, the quasi independent factors, such as organization, product and environment characteristics need also be classified in this table.

Data:

	Strategic Objectives						Organization Char.			Product Char.				Environment Char.		
	Set01 Increase market share	Set02 Increase quality	Set03 Increase stability	Set04 Increase short-term profit	Set05 Increase flexibility	Set06 Increase control	Set07 Organization size (high)	Set08 Technical experience (low)	Set09 Organizational skills (low)	Set10 Product complexity (high)	Set11 Asset specificity (high)	Set12 Strategic vulnerability (high)	Set13 Technology uncertainty (high)	Set14 Intensity of competition (high)	Set15 Market demand uncertainty (high)	Set16 Quality of business climate (low)
(A) Copy machine usage (as reference)	1	1	1	2	4	0	8	10	10	1	1	1	2	10	2	5
(B) Aircraft final assembly production	10	7	7	10	7	10	8	2	2	5	7	7	2	9	2	5
(C) Satellite rocket launch operation	10	10	7	7	5	10	8	4	6	10	10	8	4	8	4	5
(D) Space tourism rocket development	10	10	2	2	5	5	8	9	8	6	6	2	9	2	10	5
Test integration	0	10	10	0	10	10	0	0	0	10	10	10	0	0	0	10

Scale: 0 = very low; 1-3 = low; 4-6 = medium; 7-9 = high; 10 = very high

Phase 3: Define Weighting of Factors (SETTINGS Submodule)

Help: Challenging is to define the weighting of each independent factor and the relationship between strategic objectives and independent factors as a whole. Therefore, equal weighting is recommended if no better values are available.

Data:

	Strategic Objectives	Organization Char.	Product Char.	Environment Char.	Sum

Figure 17: Extract from the MoB-Tool

82 Development of a Make-or-Buy Decision-supporting Process

a) Phase 1: Define Mission Statement

Before defining the organization's strategic objectives, it is necessary to clearly define a mission statement, as shown by example in Table 13. The mission statement is assumed equal for all four case studies.

Table 13: Settings Submodule (Input Mask 1/3)

Case Study	Mission Statement
(A) Copy machine (B) Aircraft (C) Satellite (D) Space tourism	"Provide society with superior aerospace products that improve the quality of life, satisfy customer needs, and provide employees with advancement opportunities and investors with a superior rate of return."

b) Phase 2: Define Strategic Objectives and Independent Factors

Next, strategic objectives, using the mission statement as a guide (profitability, market share, quality, cost, flexibility, dependability, innovation, etc.), are defined as shown in Table 14 for each case study. In addition, quasi-independent factors, such as organization, product and environmental characteristics are also classified in this table.

Table 14: Settings Submodule (Input Mask 2/3)

Case Study	Strategic Objectives						Organization Character.			Product Character.				Environm. Character.		
	Set01 Increase market share	Set02 Increase quality	Set03 Increase stability	Set04 Increase short-term profit	Set05 Increase flexibility	Set06 Increase control	Set07 Organization size (high)	Set08 Technical experience (low)	Set09 Organizational skills (low)	Set10 Product complexity (high)	Set11 Asset specificity (high)	Set12 Strategic vulnerability (high)	Set13 Technology uncertainty (high)	Set14 Intensity of competition (high)	Set15 Market demand uncertainty (high)	Set16 Quality of business climate (low)
(A) Copy machine	1	1	1	2	4	0	8	10	10	1	1	1	2	10	2	5
(B) Aircraft	10	7	7	10	7	10	8	2	2	5	7	7	2	9	2	5
(C) Satellite	10	10	7	7	5	10	8	4	6	10	10	8	4	8	4	5
(D) Space tourism	10	10	2	2	5	5	8	9	8	6	6	2	9	2	10	6

Scale: 0 = very low; 1-3 = low; 4-6 = medium; 7-9 = high; 10 = very high

Development of a Make-or-Buy Decision-supporting Process

c) Phase 3: Define Weighting of Factors

It is challenging to define the weighting of each independent factor and the relationship between strategic objectives and independent factors as a whole. Equal weighting is assumed for all case studies (6,25%, each summing up to 100%), as shown in Table 15.

Table 15: Settings Submodule (Input Mask 3/3)

Case Study	Strategic Objectives						Organization Character.			Product Character.				Environm. Character.		
	Set01 Increase market share	Set02 Increase quality	Set03 Increase stability	Set04 Increase short-term profit	Set05 Increase flexibility	Set06 Increase control	Set07 Organization size (high)	Set08 Technical experience (low)	Set09 Organizational skills (low)	Set10 Product complexity (high)	Set11 Asset specificity (high)	Set12 Strategic vulnerability (high)	Set13 Technology uncertainty (high)	Set14 Intensity of competition (high)	Set15 Market demand uncertainty (high)	Set16 Quality of business climate (low)
(A) Copy machine	6,25	6,25	6,25	6,25	6,25	6,25	6,25	6,25	6,25	6,25	6,25	6,25	6,25	6,25	6,25	6,25
(B) Aircraft	6,25	6,25	6,25	6,25	6,25	6,25	6,25	6,25	6,25	6,25	6,25	6,25	6,25	6,25	6,25	6,25
(C) Satellite	6,25	6,25	6,25	6,25	6,25	6,25	6,25	6,25	6,25	6,25	6,25	6,25	6,25	6,25	6,25	6,25
(D) Space tourism	6,25	6,25	6,25	6,25	6,25	6,25	6,25	6,25	6,25	6,25	6,25	6,25	6,25	6,25	6,25	6,25

Note: Each row sums to 100%. Values are given in percentage (%).

d) Phase 4: Check Plausibility of Integration Pros and Outsourcing Pros Submodules

As previously noted, this is a make-or-buy decision-supporting process that is applied to the aerospace sector. Thus, assessment is done to create "Integration Pros" and "Outsourcing Pros" submodules, as shown in Table 11 and Table 12 from the aerospace sector point of view. If no better values are available, it may be possible to use this aerospace-specific data for non-aerospace sectors, but results should be analyzed carefully. In applying this process to aerospace or non-aerospace sectors, refer to Table 11 and Table 12.

e) Phase 5: Obtain Results

Vertical integration and outsourcing sub-benefits of each adjusted setting item for the four case studies are shown in Figure 18 to Figure 21.

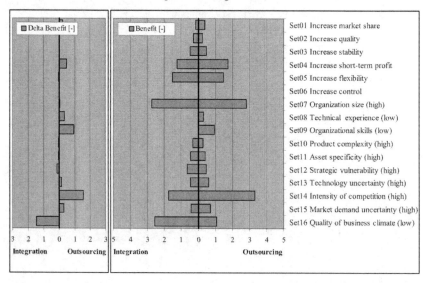

Figure 18: Sub-benefit for Case Study "(A) Copy Machine" (Res02 Output Mask)

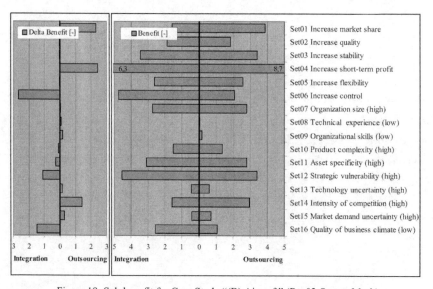

Figure 19: Sub-benefit for Case Study "(B) Aircraft" (Res02 Output Mask)

Development of a Make-or-Buy Decision-supporting Process

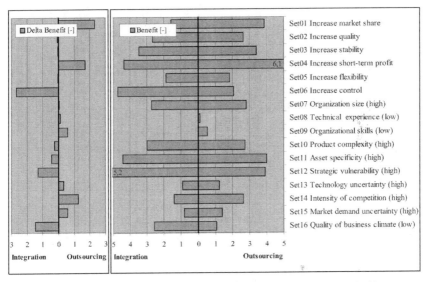

Figure 20: Sub-benefit for Case Study "(C) Satellite" (Res02 Output Mask)

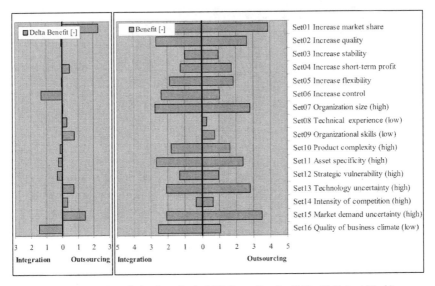

Figure 21: Sub-benefit for Case Study "(D) Space Tourism" (Res02 Output Mask)

The "Benefit" bar chart represents absolute values. Minimal values are zero and maximum values are different for each setting item. For better understanding as to whether vertical integration or outsourcing is predominant, vertical integration values are subtracted from the respective outsourcing values in the "Delta Benefit" bar chart.

Based on these (absolute) sub-benefits, Figure 22 shows the (relative) make-or-buy ratio for the four cases. The bar chart represents the ratio of "cumulated outsourcing benefit" to "cumulated vertical integration benefit," minus one for each case. The "Test integration" bar exists to test the tool against any errors in processing a vertical integration result. The input values are shown in Figure 17. In three of the four cases, the make-or-buy decision that is recommended by the tool mirrors instinctual, experience-based conclusions.

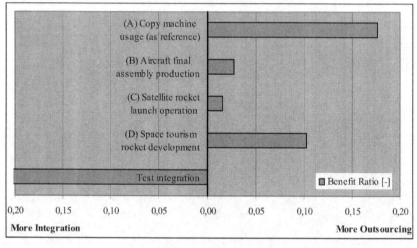

Figure 22: Outsourcing/Integration Total Benefit Ratio (Res03 Output Mask)

For case study "(A) Copy machine," as expected, the tool indicates that outsourcing of copy machine usage promises very high benefits, while vertical integration promises very low benefits; the intuitive answer is the same, as it would be an unlikely use of resources for an aerospace company to develop and build its own office copy machines. For case study "(B) Aircraft," there is no accordance between the tool and instinctual recommendation in the case of aircraft assembly; the tool showed a small preference for outsourcing, while, intuitively, the risk of revealing know-how to outside producers

Development of a Make-or-Buy Decision-supporting Process 87

would lead one to suggest integrating this activity. For case study "(C) Satellite," the tool shows a tendency toward recommending outsourcing the operation of rockets, rather than integrating it. The case study from Chapter 2 led to the same result. For case study "(D) Space tourism," the results show that there is a significant benefit to outsourcing the development of a space tourism rocket. This also makes intuitive sense, because the daily operations attendant necessary to make near-term profits would not blend well with the futuristic creativity (and far-term profit) that such a program requires.

Results of Case A, C and D reflect expectations, while Case B does not. Reasons for this might include: (1) expectations are incorrect and it is actually better to outsource an aircraft's final assembly production; (2) the process characteristics are based on incorrect assumptions; and/or (3) important information from the case study is not included in the input mask. An empirical validation in the form of expert interviews might help to more clearly identify these reasons.

4.4 Discussion

4.4.1 General

The following section attempts to widen the study's point of view through a discussion centered on: (1) the choice of items for the "Setting" submodule; (2) the sensitivity of propositions of the "Integration Pros" and "Outsourcing Pros" submodule; (3) a trade-off between informal and formal statements; (4) a comparison between processes and/or models from other authors to my developed make-or-buy decision-supporting process; and (5) limitations concerning the introduced process.

4.4.2 Choice of Items for "Settings" Submodule

The balanced scorecard philosophy is used to create the "Setting" submodule. The balanced scorecard, introduced by Kaplan and Norton (1992), is a widely used strategic business performance measurement system. This method seeks to report on leading indicators of an organization's health, rather than referring to traditional accounting measures alone. These leading indicators are called Key Performance Indicators (KPI) because they are critical to the successful execution of an organization's strategy. Based on the strategic goals of an organization, target values for KPIs are set. KPIs enable an organization to measure and monitor its performance on a strategic and operational level. The goal is to establish a common KPI language that spans all areas of an enterprise.

Typically, KPIs are used in a post-ante context to evaluate an organization's past performance. Krauth et al. (2005) reason that KPIs should be utilized in the planning phase as well, thus ex-ante. I follow this approach for the make-or-buy decision-supporting process. A key attribute of this process is its support for identifying causal linkages between components of the business that fulfill the strategy (i.e., to determine the benefit share of each proposition that contributes to either vertical integration or outsourcing).

Often the balanced scorecard is broken down into a financial, customer, process and an HR & innovation perspective. This procedure aims to avoid the classic problems of measurement, such as (Van Aken & Coleman, 2002) use of too many metrics, use of exclusively cost metrics, use of only short-term focused metrics and use of metrics that drive the wrong behaviors.

The choice of KPIs is organization-specific and depends upon its goals. An organization's goals change over time (Allio, 2006). In a start-up high technology company, for example, managers focus on reliability. In the growth stage, managers concentrate on market share. In mature industries, managers focus on production costs and/or capacity utilization. In an aging industry, managers primarily focus on cash flow. I select those KPIs for the make-or-buy decision that I recommend for use by a typically mature aerospace organization. Due to the modularity of this process, it can be extended easily to additional KPIs and/or existing KPIs can be terminated. In addition, my proposed weighting (I assume equal weighting) of each KPI is easily changeable.

4.4.3 Sensitivity Analysis

I perform sensitivity analysis to make the process properties more transparent; helping to identify critical elements and interpret estimation results. Saltelli, Tarantola, Campolongo and Ratto (2004) define sensitivity analysis as the study of how the uncertainty in the output of a model (numerical or otherwise) can be apportioned to different sources of uncertainty in the model input. Each input factor is perturbed, in turn, while keeping all other input factors fixed at their nominal value (i.e., the "One-factor-at-a-Time" approach), to determine its influence on the result: e.g., the effect on the make-or-buy result for a very low and a very high value of item "Set04 Increase short-term

Development of a Make-or-Buy Decision-supporting Process

profit." I assume that a sensitivity analysis based on the "One-factor-at-a-Time" approach delivers sufficiently significant results for a linear, equation-based process, as developed in this study.

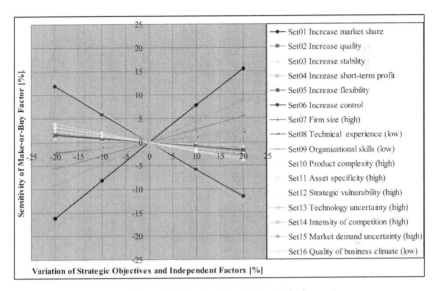

Figure 23: Result of Sensitivity Analysis

I use the data set of the case study "(D) Space tourism rocket development" for sensitivity analysis. The result is shown in Figure 23. All values are within the acceptable range and no anomalies are found. "Set01 Increase market share," "Set06 Increase control" and "Set16 Quality of business climate (low)" sensitivities are higher than +/-10% when strategic objectives and independent factors are varied +/-20%. Thus, special attention should be paid when these values are set.

4.4.4 Informal Versus Formal Statements

Some readers may prefer or expect formal statements to informal ones. I choose to use informal statements for two reasons.

First, characteristics of aerospace organizations are unique compared to the overall characteristics of most other industries as shown in Chapter 2. For this reason, many economic theories should be modified to apply to the special cases of aerospace organizations (Goehlich & Bebenroth, 2008). Dealing with those theories from a qualitative view (i.e., using informal statements) rather than a quantitative view (i.e., using formal statements), makes it easier to determine the potential and weaknesses of investigated theories, items and propositions.

Second, my motivation and attempt is to generate an overall make-or-buy decision-supporting process for aerospace organizations toward understanding the commonalities, distinctions and interactions of the (normally isolated watched) make-or-buy theories and known recommendations. Furthermore, I am motivated to provide a combined account of the costs, risks and benefits of outsourcing versus vertical integration. To accomplish this, I discover that the top-down approach of using informal statements is superior to the bottom-up approach of using formal statements: simulating the complex architecture of aerospace organizations by only formal statements would cause a disaster due to the overwhelmingly unmanageable number of equations it would create. Use of informal statements permits the necessary distance required for the "battlefield of theories" and allows me to uncover important coherences. This is in accordance with Gibbons (2005, p. 236), who states that "firms have invented far more ways to work together than organizational economics has so far expressed (not to mention evaluated)" combined with Krugman's (1995, p. 54) warning for "sensible ideas that could not be effectively formalized [and] formalizable ideas that seem to have missed the point." Further consideration can be found in Baker, Gibbons and Murphy (2004).

4.4.5 Comparison With Other Studies

Many authors investigate business cases for outsourcing. Due to very different assumptions in these studies, an exact comparison is not possible at this time. However, a preliminary comparison is attempted in order to enlarge the basis of discussion for make-or-buy decision models and/or processes. Several models are drawn in the economic literature to distinguish between activities that can be outsourced and those that should be made in-house by the buyer based on multiple criteria. Some of the models sorted by year of publication are listed below:

- The Tullock (1980) model, based on rent-seeking, allows one to determine the transaction costs of outsourcing, but does not produce a trade-off between outsourcing and vertical integration.

Development of a Make-or-Buy Decision-supporting Process

- The Venkatesan (1992) model indicates that there are either core products that should be strictly produced in house or non-core products that should be strictly produced with the help of suppliers. The weakness of this model is its neglect of the intermediate types of products (from core to non-core) and thus, the corresponding recommendations.

- The Quinn and Hilmer (1995) model is based on the dimensions "degree of strategic vulnerability" and "potential for competitive advantage." This model covers three conditions of make-or-buy (in-house production, partnership and buy-off-the-shelf). The authors only analyze some possibilities out of a total of nine.

- The Olsen and Ellram (1997) model specializes in the partnership condition and distinguishes between strategic products (important, but difficult to manage), bottle-neck products (not important and difficult to manage) and leverage products (important and easy to manage). In-house production and buy-off-the-shelf are not considered.

- The Clemons and Hitt (1997) model is based on the concept of a "keeper." An activity should be considered "a keeper" if its loss, should it occur, would entail high costs or even destroy the company. Clemons and Hitt argue that the traditional characterization of "core" is of little use in assessing what can be outsourced. Instead they propose the formation of the following four groups: (1) Strategic Competence: an activity that represents a keeper and a competence that should not be outsourced. (2) Strategic Incompetence: an activity that represents a keeper, but is poorly performed internally should not be outsourced. Outsourcing would initially offer benefits, but the potential losses of outsourcing will dominate any short-term gains. Instead, these incompetence activities should be improved. (3) Non-strategic Competence: an activity that represents a non-keeper, but is a company's competence and can be outsourced or become a business unit. (4) Non-strategic incompetence: an activity that represents a non-keeper and an incompetence that should be outsourced. Outsourcing offers opportunities for performance improvement with moderate risks.

- The Levin and Tadelis (2005) model distinguishes between various contract forms that range from employment, and thus vertical integration, to outsourcing types. This model's feature is to investigate the make-or-buy decision from the point of contracts.

In an enhancement to existing models, the process developed in the present study covers the entire spectrum of make-or-buy decisions (the continuum from in-house to buy-off-the-shelf). This means that existing models are isolated, as they do not take into consideration the parameters developed by one another. The strengths of this developed process are to support the decision-makers with holistic recommendations. It focuses on improvement to explain and predict organizational architecture from an economic-efficiency perspective. The process allows one to determine what organizational (and supplier) architecture is best suited to a specified activity. The economic environment is held fixed for analyzing alternative structures individually, and finally compared to one another.

4.4.6 Limitations

Extant make-or-buy related studies are quite voluminous. Thus, complete implementation of this literature into the make-or-buy decision-supporting process is beyond the scope of the present study. Rather, I limit my discussions and investigations on those studies that I found to have significant influence on make-or-buy decisions, especially for managers. However, I find that many extant studies suffer from measurement problems, such as follows:

- Some factors, such as motivational, cultural and social factors are hard to handle, but may strongly influence decisions.

- Several studies examine only one factor that is predicted to affect the make-or-buy decision, holding other factors constant, whereas it is often a combination of such factors that should be assessed (Lafontaine & Slade, 2007).

- While it is easy to determine external transaction costs (buyer to supplier) but difficult to identify internal transaction costs (department to department), many results of trade-off studies are unjustified, biased in favor of vertical integration. However, those companies who conduct extensive outsourcing may have too many suppliers. This would be more costly to manage than less efficient in-house operations, as argued by Blaxill and Hout (1991).

- Companies from different countries generally apply divergent success criteria because of unique cultures (Yan & Zeng, 1999). In addition, each culture has specific cultural codes, e.g., the trust-based cooperative norms of Japanese society encourage

Development of a Make-or-Buy Decision-supporting Process

high collaboration rates among companies (Todeva & Knoke, 2005). Thus, assessing international scenarios is especially complicated because results are biased by different cultural environments.

- A challenge exists whether to use objective outcome indicators (e.g., financial gains, number of innovations, revenue), subjective indicators (e.g., partner satisfaction with the collaboration, customer service, corporate identity) or both, in order to fully assess the performance of organizations.

- In the case of the make-or-buy decision-supporting process, some of the propositions overlap each other partly or one proposition may be a sub-proposition of another (e.g., proposition "Out11 Reduce labor costs" is to a great extent a sub-proposition of proposition "Out17 Reduce production costs"). Avoiding this fact would result in garbling of the modules. Instead, double counting of similar advantages is avoided in the present study by carefully assigning values to each proposition (e.g., the benefit value of proposition "Out17 Reduce production costs" excludes the benefit of low labor costs, as this item is represented by proposition "Out11 Reduce labor costs").

Thus, the precision of propositions is limited. Yet, I assume that a preponderance of indication, gathered across plentiful studies of diverse industries, time periods and geographic regions using different approaches, yields convincing evidence as to the validity of the introduced make-or-buy decision-supporting process.

4.5 Results

The purpose of this chapter is to investigate make-or-buy decisions. The primary output is the development of a process as well as its application to four case studies. The process provides a tool, based on theories, empirical data and systematic means that is designed to support managers in generating make-or-buy decisions of greater accuracy and transparency than is currently available.

Although strategic motives for organizations to engage either in vertical integration or in outsourcing vary according to the setting (organization-specific characteristics, product characteristics, multiple environmental factors, etc.), it is possible to observe significant results.

The present findings have important managerial implications. First, results confirm that make-or-buy decisions are important contributors to control, stability and coordination aspects of business decisions. Second, one can see that effective make-or-buy decision expertise is critical to an organization's success. Third, the process shows that scattering the main question (i.e., the make-or-buy decision) into many sub-questions (i.e., the 16 items and 47 propositions), helps to generate a transparent and strategy-oriented solution.

The next step, but beyond the scope of the present study, is an empirical validation of the tool in the form of interviews with aerospace experts, economists and politicians.

5 Conclusion

This chapter summarizes the results of the three studies discussed in Chapters 2, 3 and 4. Detailed discussions and specific results can be found in the discussion and results sections of each main chapter. Here, I highlight the key outcomes of this research series:

- In Chapter 2, the characteristics of aerospace organizations are shown as unique compared to those of most other industries.

  High market power for most types of aerospace organizations, highly complex systems, high outsourcing ratio trends, large military market shares, strong government financial support and challenging assessment of performance are all unique characteristics. This part of the study also shows that the aviation and space sectors share many features (e.g., high quality standards, massive entry costs, very low production rates, high strategic power and high degree of internationalization) that are nearly identical, while other features (e.g., market structure, demand-supply interactions, unit size of production and imperfect competition) are different.

  I conclude in Chapter 2 that other extreme sectors, such as the oil rig sector, the World Wide Web sector and the shipbuilding sector, have some unique and some similar characteristics to the aerospace sector. An investigation into those sectors is not in the scope of the present study but may be a fruitful area for future research.

- Chapter 3 establishes that many economic theories should be modified if applied to the cases of aerospace organizations.

  Thus, one should study the make-or-buy recommendations from consultants with caution as their results are typically based on general assumptions and conventional economic theories, not those specific to the aerospace sector. I demonstrate in my research on space organizations the reasons that the Japanese government's activities in this industry have shifted toward using private companies, a shift that has also been visible in both Europe and the USA in recent years.

  As an example, I show that the aim of the Japanese space organization JAXA is to increase the competitiveness of Japanese commercial launch services but, to do this, JAXA needs to reduce costs, increase reliability, and improve customer service. Under the current organizational architecture (i.e., where basic research, production and operating divisions are vertically integrated), the ability of this organization to increase its commercial competitiveness is significantly limited. However, the development toward outsourcing launch operation activities cannot be explained by either transaction cost theory or the human resource-based view, but is congruent with the agency theory.

With *transaction cost theory*, outsourcing would result in higher transaction costs than would vertical integration activities, especially when the environment is uncertain, and assets are specific and heavily used. In the *human resource-based view*, advantages accrue when activities are efficiently vertically integrated because outsourcing depletes human resource knowledge. Thus, JAXA's outsourcing is more in accord with *agency theory*, where outsourcing activities for space organizations are preferable over vertical integration when the costs of misalignment conflicts caused by outsourcing are lower than the costs of the incentives from vertical integration.

Therefore, the directional trend of outsourcing activities in space organizations is most congruent with principal-agent theory; transaction cost theory and the human resource-based view both fail to provide sufficient reasons to explain why JAXA should vertically integrate its activities to be more efficient, rather than outsourcing them to private companies.

I conclude in Chapter 3 that conventional, broad-based economic theories have only limited application to the space sector – and possibly the aviation sector as well. To corroborate this conclusion, other similar space and/or aviation-specific case studies should be tested using these three theories. Further, the extent to which each of these theories may have proportionate or disproportionate influence on the theoretical results is a difficult task and a challenge for future research.

- Chapter 4 develops a tool that facilitates make-or-buy decisions for managers working in the aerospace sector.

    About 50 propositions of make-or-buy decisions, mostly gained from secondary analysis, are collected and ranked. Then those propositions are systematically connected to 6 strategic objectives, 3 organizational characteristics, 4 product characteristics and 3 environmental characteristics.

    The resulting tool is applied to four case studies taken from the aerospace sector: (A) Copy machine usage (as a reference), (B) Aircraft final assembly production,

Conclusion

(C) Satellite rocket launch operation and (D) Space tourism rocket development. In three of the four cases, the make-or-buy decision recommended by the tool mirrored instinctual, experience-based conclusions.

Case (A): As expected, the tool indicates that outsourcing of copy machine usage promises very high benefits, while vertical integration promises very low benefits; the intuitive answer is the same, as it would be an unlikely use of resources for an aerospace company to develop and build its own office copy machines.

Case (B): There is no accordance between the tool and instinctual recommendation in the case of aircraft assembly; the tool showed a small preference for outsourcing, while, intuitively, the risk of revealing know-how to outside producers would lead one to suggest integrating this activity.

Case (C): The tool shows a tendency toward recommending outsourcing the operation of rockets, rather than integrating it. The case study from Chapter 2 led to the same result.

Case (D): The results show that there is a significant benefit to outsourcing the development of a space tourism rocket. This also makes intuitive sense, because the daily operations attendant to making near-term profit would not blend well with the futuristic creativity (and far-term profit) that such a program requires.

I conclude in Chapter 4 that the main outcome of this study is the development of a make-or-buy decision-supporting process. A structured application procedure makes this process attractive to any manager who needs a simple and transparent tool to support make-or-buy decisions. Dividing the make-or-buy question into many sub-questions based on, in this case, 16 objectives and characteristics, helps decision-makers generate a transparent and strategy-oriented solution with fair attention to all important considerations. By contrast, the less structured intuitive approach allows the decision-maker to weigh only a few arguments/propositions simultaneously – typically those which have current subjective importance for the decider, e.g., bad news about Dollar/Euro currency trends, which would favor an outsourcing decision or bad news about risk of revealing know-how, which would favor an integration decision as in Case (B). The next step, which is beyond the scope of the present study, is an empirical validation of the tool in the form of interviews with aerospace experts, economists and politicians.

As closing thought, from these three studies, I have concluded that economic motivational goals, political hurdles and technical challenges should be more closely merged in the early phases of strategic decision-making for any new, large-scale program in aerospace organizations. By doing so, decision-makers can adapt the organizational architecture of aerospace organizations to the needs of any planned big program, resulting in an important aspect of efficiency improvements.

References

A.T. Kearney (2003). "The Shifting Roles of Suppliers," http://www.atkearney.com, Author, Chicago, accessed: 15.5.2008.

Airbus (2008). "Global Market Forecast 2007-2026," http://www.airbus.com/en/corporate/gmf, Author, Toulouse, accessed: 10.2.2008.

Akerlof, G.A. (1970). "The Market for Lemons: Quality Uncertainty and the Market Mechanism," *The Quarterly Journal of Economics*, Vol. 84, No. 3, pp. 488-500.

Alchian, A. (1963). "Reliability of Progress Curves in Airframe Production," *Econometrica*, Vol. 31, No. 4, pp. 679-693.

Alexander, C. & M.I. Marshall (2006). "The Risk Matrix: Illustrating the Importance of Risk Management Strategies," *Journal of Extension*, Vol. 44, No. 2, Article 2TOT1.

Allio, M. (2006). "Metrics that matter: seven guidelines for better performance measurement," *Handbook of Business Strategy*, Vol. 7, No. 1, pp. 255-263.

Anderson, E. & D.C. Schmittlein (1984). "Integration of the Sales Force: An Empirical Examination," *RAND Journal of Economics*, Vol. 15, No. 3, pp. 385-395.

Anderson, L. (1999). "Impact of Aviation on the Economy," presented to the NRC Committee on Strategic Assessment of US Aeronautics, June 1999, NASA Glenn Research Center, Cleveland, OH.

Anselmo, J.C. (2005). "Top of Their Game," *Aviation Week & Space Technology*, 6 June Issue, McGraw-Hill Aerospace & Defense, New York, pp. 45-51.

Aoki, M. (1988). *Information, Incentives, and Bargaining in the Japanese Economy*, Cambridge University Press, Cambridge, MA.

Arend, H. (1987). "Systemanalyse und Kostenoptimierung wiederverwendbarer ballistischer Trägerraketen," Doctoral Thesis, Technical University Berlin, Berlin.

Argote, L., S. Beckman & D. Epple (1990). "The Persistence and Transfer of Learning in Industrial Settings," *Management Science*, Vol. 36, No. 2, pp. 140-154.

Arianespace (2007). "About Arianespace," http://www.arianespace.com, Author, Evry-Courcouronnes, France, accessed: 17.9.2007.

Arrow, K.J. (1969). "The Organization of Economic Activity: Issues Pertinent to the Choice of Market versus Nonmarket Allocation," in: *The Analysis and Evaluation of Public Expenditures: The PPB System*, Vol. 1, Joint Economic Committee, Washington D.C., pp. 47-64.

Arrow, K.J. (1970). *Essays in the Theory of Risk-bearing*, North-Holland, Amsterdam.

Asahi Shinbun (2007). "衛星ビジネス発射　三菱重、Ｈ２Ａ打ち上げ成功 (H-2A satellite launch lift-up business by Mitsubishi Heavy was a success)," 15 September, http://www.asahi.com/special/space/TKY200709150012.html, Author, Tokyo, accessed: 26.9.2007.

Aubert, B., S. Rivard & M. Patry (1996). "A Transaction Cost Approach to Outsourcing Behavior," *Information Management*, Vol. 30, pp. 51-64.

Babbie, E. (2000). *The Practice of Social Research*, 9th Edition, Wadsworth/Thomson Learning, Belmont, CA.

Baker, G., R. Gibbons & K.J. Murphy (2004). "Strategic alliances: bridges between 'islands of conscious power'," Working Paper, Harvard Business School, Boston.

Barnard, C.I. (1938). *The Functions of the Executive*, Harvard University Press, Cambridge, MA.

References

101

Bean, L. (2003). "The Profits and Perils of International Outsourcing," *The Journal of Corporate Accounting & Finance*, pp. 3-10.

Becht, M., P. Bolton & A. Roell (2003). "Corporate Governance and Control," in: Constantinides, G.M., M. Harris & R.M. Stulz (Eds.), *Handbook of the Economics of Finance*, Vol. 1, Elsevier, Amsterdam, pp. 1-109.

Benkard, C.L. (2000). "Learning and Forgetting: The Dynamics of Aircraft Production," *The American Economic Review*, Vol. 90, No. 4, pp. 1034-1054.

Benkard, C.L. (2004). "A Dynamic Analysis of the Market for Wide-Bodied Commercial Aircraft," *Review of Economic Studies*, Vol. 71, No. 3, pp. 581-611.

Bennett, M.M. (1997). "Strategic Alliances in the World Airline Industry," *Progress in Tourism and Hospitality Research Journal*, Vol. 3, pp. 213-223.

Bental, B. & D. Demougin (2006). "Incentive Contracts and Total Factor Productivity," *International Economic Review*, Vol. 47, No. 3, pp. 1033-1055.

Berger, P. & E. Ofek (1995). "Diversification's Effect on Firm Value," *Journal of Financial Economics*, Vol. 37, pp. 39-65.

Berndt, E.R., A.F. Friedlaender & J. Wang Chiang (1990). "Interdependent Pricing and Markup Behavior: An Empirical Analysis of GM, Ford and Chrysler," NBER Working Paper, No. W3396, MIT, Cambridge, MA.

Blaxill, M.F. & T.M. Hout (1991). "The fallacy of the overhead quick fix," *Harvard Business Review*, July-August, pp. 93-101.

Boeing (2007a). "Current Market Outlook 2007," http://www.boeing.com/commercial /cmo/pdf/Boeing_Current_Market_Outlook_2007.pdf, Author, Seattle, WA, accessed: 11.2.2008.

Boeing (2007b). "Full Year Results 2006," http://www.boeing.com/companyoffices/ financial/quarterly.htm, Author, Huntington Beach, CA, accessed: 8.6.2007.

Boeing (2008). "Boeing Launch Services," http://www.boeing.com/defense-space/space, Author, Huntington Beach, CA, accessed: 10.8.2008.

Brickley, J.A., C.W. Smith & J.L. Zimmerman (2006). *Managerial Economics and Organizational Architecture*, Fourth Edition, McGraw-Hill, New York.

Burgers, W.P., C.W.L. Hill & W. Chan Kim (1996). "A Theory of Global Strategic Alliances: The Case of the Global Auto Industry," *Strategic Management Journal*, Vol. 14, No. 6, pp. 419-432.

Business Environment Risk Intelligence (2005). "Risk Ratings, Analyses, and Forecasts for over 140 Countries," http://www.beri.com, Author, Friday Harbor, WA, accessed: 27.1.2008.

Carlton, D. & M. Klamer (1983). "The Need for Coordination among Firms with Special Reference to Network Industries," *University of Chicago Law Review*, Vol. 50, pp. 446-465.

Chen, M. (2004). Asian Management Systems, Second Edition, *Thomson Learning*, Boston.

Chen, Z. & T.W. Ross (2000). "Strategic alliances, shared facilities, and entry deterrence," *RAND Journal of Economics*, Vol. 31, No. 2, pp. 326-344.

Clemons, E.K. & L.M. Hitt (1997). "Strategic Sourcing for Services: Assessing the Balance between Outsourcing and Insourcing," Working Paper, University of Pennsylvania, Philadelphia, PA.

Coase, R.H. (1937). "The Nature of the Firm," *Economica*, Vol. 4, pp. 386-405.

References

Commission on Engineering and Technical Systems (1999). "Recent Trends in U.S. Aeronautics Research and Technology," http://www.aerostates.org/ASA_files/NatAcad.pdf, Aerospace States Association (ASA), Arlington, VA, accessed: 3.9.2007.

Crocker, K.J. & K.J. Reynolds (1993). "The Efficiency of Incomplete Contracts: An Empirical Analysis of Air Force Engine Procurement," *RAND Journal of Economics*, Vol. 24, pp. 126-146.

Cyert, R.M. & J.G. March (1963). *A Behavioural Theory of the Firm*, Prentice Hall, Englewood Cliffs, NJ.

David, D. (1985). "R&D Consortia," High Technology, p. 42.

David, L. (2002). "New ISS Study Warns of Increased Operating Costs," http://www.space.com/news/spacestation/rand_study_020219.html, Space.com, New York, accessed: 30.8.2007.

Defense Federal Acquisition Regulation Supplement (2006). "The 1998 Edition," DoD, Washington D.C., revised 2006, p. 32-069.

Destefani, J. (2004). "A Look at Boeing's Outsourcing Strategy," *Manufacturing Engineering*, Vol. 132, No. 3, pp. 65-73.

Domberger, S. (1998). *The Contracting Organization: A Strategic Guide to Outsourcing*, Oxford University Press, Oxford.

Downs, A. (1966). *Bureaucratic Structure and Decisionmaking*, Rand Corporation, Santa Monica, CA.

EADS (2007). "Year 2006 Report: Unaudited Condensed Consolidated Financial Information of EADS N.V. for the year 2006," http://www.eads.net/1024/en/investor/Reports/Financial_Statements.html, Author, Le Carre, The Netherlands, accessed: 14.3.2007.

Engardio, P., A. Bernstein & M. Kripalani (2003). "The new global job shift: The next round of globalization is sending upscale jobs offshore," *Business Week*, 3 February, pp. 50-60.

ESA (2006). "Agenda 2011 – A Document by the Director General and Directors," *esa bulletin 128*, Author, Paris, p. 8.

Esty, B. (2004). "Airbus A3XX: Developing the World's Largest Commercial Jet (A)," HBS Case 9-201-028, Harvard Business School, Boston.

Euromonitor International (2005). "Aerospace in the USA," Industry Reports, Author, London.

Federal Acquisition Regulation (2005). "FAR Reissue Volume 1," General Service Administration, DoD and NASA, Washington D.C., pp. 16.2-1 & 16.4-2.

Flath, D. (1980). "The Economics of Short-Term Leasing," *Economic Inquiry*, Vol. 18, pp. 247-259.

Frynas, G, K. Mellahi & G. Pigman (2006). "First Mover-Advantages in International Business and Firm-Specific Political Resources," *Strategic Management Journal*, Vol. 27, pp. 321-345.

Geringer, M. (1988). *Joint venture partner selection: Strategies for developed countries*, Quorum Books, New York.

Gerlach, M.L. (1997). *Alliance Capitalism: The Social Organization of Japanese Business*, University of California Press, Berkeley, CA.

Gibbons, R. (2005). "Four formal(izable) theories of the firm?" *Journal of Economic Behavior and Organization*, Vol. 58, pp. 200-245.

Goehlich, R.A. (2002). *Space Tourism: Economic and Technical Evaluation of Suborbital Space Flight for Tourism*, Der Andere Verlag, Osnabrueck, Germany.

References 105

Goehlich, R.A. (2005). "A Ticket pricing strategy for an oligopolistic space tourism market," *Space Policy Journal*, Vol. 21, No. 4, pp. 293-306.

Goehlich, R.A. & R. Bebenroth (2008). "Outsourcing Strategies in Europe, USA and Japan: A Case of Space Organizations," 国民経済雑誌 *(The Kukumin-Keizai Zasshi: Journal of Economics & Business Administration)*, Vol. 197, No. 3, pp. 75-89.

Goehlich, R.A. & U. Ruecker (2005). "Low-cost Management Aspects for Developing, Producing and Operating Future Space Transportation Systems," *Acta Astronautica Journal*, Vol. 56, No. 1-2, pp. 337-346.

Goldstein, A. (2002). "The Political Economy of High-tech Industries in Developing Countries: Aerospace in Brazil, Indonesia and South Africa," *Cambridge Journal of Economics*, Vol. 26, No. 4, pp. 521-538.

Grob, R. (1984). *Erweiterte Wirtschaftlichkeits- und Nutzenrechnung: Duale Bewertung von Maßnahmen zur Arbeitsgestaltung*; TÜV Rheinland, Köln, Germany.

Grossman, S.J. & O.D. Hart (1986). "The Costs and Benefits of Ownership: A Theory of Vertical and Lateral Integration," *Journal of Political Economy*, Vol. 94, No. 4, pp. 691-719.

Grossman, G.M. & E. Helpman (2002). "Integration versus Outsourcing in Industry Equilibrium," *Quarterly Journal of Economics*, Vol. 117, pp. 85-120.

Grossman, G.M. & E. Helpman (2004). "Managerial incentives and the international organization of production," *Journal of International Economics*, Vol. 63, pp. 237-262.

Grout, P.A. (1984). "Investment and Wages in the Absence of Binding Contracts: A Nash Bargaining Approach," *Econometrica*, Vol. 52, No. 2, pp. 449-460.

Hague, L. (2003). "Global Launch Services Prospects in a declining Commercial Satellite Market," Boeing Launch Services, AIAA 2003-6409, presented at *Space 2003 Conference*, Long Beach, CA.

Harrigan, K.R. (1984). "Formulating Vertical Integration Strategies," *The Academy of Management Review*, Vol. 9, No. 4, pp. 638-652.

Hart, O. (1995). *Firms, Contracts, and Financial Structure*, Oxford University Press, Oxford.

Hart, O., J. Tirole, D.W. Carlton & O.E. Williamson (1990). "Vertical Integration and Market Foreclosure," *Brookings Papers on Economic Activity*, Vol. 1990, pp. 205-286.

Hayek, F.A. (1945). "The Use of Knowledge in Society," *The American Economic Review*, Vol. 35, No. 4, pp. 519-530.

Heide, J.B. & G. John (1988). "The Role of Dependence Balancing in Safeguarding Transaction-Specific Assets in Conventional Channels," *Journal of Marketing*, Vol. 52, pp. 20-35.

Heinemann, K. (2007). "Mit dem geleasten Jet durchstarten: Flugzeugleasing ist eine boomende Branche – Bis 2010 sind für Kunden kaum noch Maschinen zu haben," *Handelsblatt*, No. 199, 16 October, p. B7.

Hollensen, S. (2007). *Global Marketing - A Decision-Oriented Approach*, Financial Times Prent.Int, London, p. 251.

Holmstrom, B. (1999). "The Firm as a Subeconomy," *Journal of Law, Economics and Organization*, Vol. 15, pp. 74-102.

Holmstrom, B. & P. Milgrom (1991). "Multitask-Principal-Agent Analyses: Incentive Contracts, Asset Ownership, and Job Design," *Journal of Law, Economics and Organization*, Vol. 7, Special Issue, pp. 24-52.

References

Irwin, D.A. & N. Pavcnik (2004). "Airbus versus Boeing revisited: international competition in the aircraft market," *Journal of International Economics*, Vol. 64, pp. 223-245.

JAXA (2005). "JAXA Vision 2025," http://www.jaxa.jp/about/vision_missions/long_term/jaxa_vision_e.pdf, Author, Tokyo, accessed: 17.9.2007.

Jensen, M.C. (1986). "Agency Costs of Free Cash Flow, Corporate Finance, and Takeovers," *American Economic Review*, Vol. 76, pp. 323-329.

Jensen, M.C. & W.H. Meckling (1976). "Theory of the firm: Managerial behavior, agency costs and ownership structure," *Journal of Financial Economics*, Vol. 3, No. 4, pp. 305-360.

Jensen, P.H. & R.E. Stonecash (2005). "Contract Efficiency in the Presence of Demand and Cost Uncertainty," Working Paper, No. 1/05, The University of Melbourne, Melbourne.

Kamath, R.R. & J.K. Liker (1994). "A second look at Japanese product development," *Havard Business Review*, pp. 154-170.

Kaplan, R.S. & D.P. Norton (1992). "The Balanced Scorecard – Measures that Drives Performance," *Harvard Business Review*, Vol. 75, No. 2, pp. 70-79.

Klein, B., R.G. Crawford & A.A. Alchian (1978). "Vertical Integration, Appropriable Rents, and the Competitive Contracting Process," *Journal of Law and Economics*, Vol. 21, No. 2, pp. 297-326.

Koelle, D.E. (2003). *Handbook of Cost Engineering for Space Transportation Systems with Transcost 7.1*, TCS – TransCostSystems, Ottobrunn, Germany.

Krauth E., H. Moonen, V. Popova & M. Schut (2005). "Performance measurement and control in logistics service providing," *The Icfaian Journal of Management Research*, Vol. 4, No. 7, pp. 7-19.

Krugman, P. (1995). *Development, Geography and Economic Theory*, MIT Press, Cambridge, MA.

Lafontaine, F. & M. Slade (2007). "Vertical Integration and Firm Boundaries: The Evidence," *Journal of Economic Literature*, Vol. 45, No. 3, pp. 629-685.

Lau, R. (1994). "Why everyone wants to know more about strategic alliances," *Broker World*, Vol. 14, No. 2, pp. 48-54.

Levin, J. & S. Tadelis (2005). "Employment versus contracting in procurement: theory and evidence from U.S. cities," presented at Econometric Society World Congress (ESWC) 2005, 19-24 August, London.

Levine, D.I. & L.A. Tyson (1990). "Participation, Productivity, and the Firm's Environment," in: Blinder, A.S. (Ed.), *Paying for Productivity: A Look at the Evidence*, The Brookings Institution, Washington D.C., pp. 183-237.

Lorell, M.A. & H.P. Levaux (1998). "The Cutting Edge: A Half Century of U.S. Fighter Aircraft R&D," Issue Paper MR-939-AF, RAND, Santa Monica, CA.

Lynn, M. (1998). *Birds of Prey: Boeing vs. Airbus: A Battle for the Skies*, Four Walls Eight Windows, New York.

MacPherson, A. & D. Pritchard (2002). "The International Decentralization of US Commercial Aircraft Production: Implications for US Employment and Trade," Occasional Paper No. 26, Canada-United States Trade Center, Buffalo, NY.

MacPherson, A. & D. Pritchard (2007). "Boeing's Diffusion of Commercial Aircraft Technology to Japan: Surrendering the US Industry for Foreign Financial Support," *Journal of Labor Research*, Vol. 28, No. 3, pp. 552-566.

Mahnke, V. (2001). "The Process of Vertical Dis-Integration: An Evolutionary Perspective on Outsourcing," *Journal of Management and Governance*, Vol. 5, pp. 353-379.

References 109

Majd, S. & S.C. Myers (1987). "Tax Asymmetries and Corporate Income Tax Reform," in: Feldstein, M. (Ed.), *Effects of Taxation on Capital Accumulation*, University of Chicago Press, Chicago.

Malerba, F. & L. Orsenigo (1995). "Schumpeterian Patterns of Innovation," *Cambridge Journal of Economics*, Vol. 19, pp. 47-65.

Manabat, C.L. (2003). "The financial executive," *BusinessWorld*, 3 April, p. 1.

Masten, S. (1984). "The Organization of Production: Evidence from the Aerospace Industry," *Journal of Law and Economics*, Vol. 27, No. 2, pp. 403-417.

Masten, S. (1988). "A legal basis for the firm," *Journal of Law, Economics and Organization*, Vol. 4, pp. 181-198.

Mattsson, L.G. (1995). "International strategies: a network approach," in: Faulkner, D. (Ed.), *International Strategic Alliances*, McGraw-Hill, London.

McAfee, R.P. & J. McMillan (1995). "Organizational Diseconomies of Scale," *Journal of Economics and Management Strategy*, Vol. 4, No. 3, pp. 399-426.

McGuire, S. (2006). "The United States, Japan and the Aerospace Industry: technological change in the shaping of a political relationship," Working Paper, University of Bath, Bath, United Kingdom.

Milgrom, P.R. (1988). "Employment Contracts, Influence Activities, and Efficient Organization Design," *The Journal of Political Economy*, Vol. 96, pp. 42-60.

Milgrom, P.R. & J. Roberts (1988). "An economic approach to influence activities in organizations," *The American Journal of Sociology*, Vol. 94, pp. 154-179.

Miller, M.H. & C.W. Upton (1976). "Leasing, Buying, and the Cost of Capital Services," *The Journal of Finance*, Vol. 31, No. 3, pp. 761-786.

Mitsubishi Heavy Industries (2007). "H-IIA Launch Services," Space Systems Department, http://www.h2a.jp, Author, Tokyo, accessed: 17.9.2007.

Monteverde, K. & D.J. Teece (1982a). "Appropriable Rents and Quasi-Vertical Integration," *Journal of Law and Economics*, Vol. 25, No. 2, pp. 321-328.

Monteverde, K. & D.J. Teece (1982b). "Supplier Switching Costs and Vertical Integration in the Automobile Industry," *The Bell Journal of Economics*, Vol. 13, pp. 206-213.

Mullins, D.W. (1982). "Does the Capital Asset Pricing Model Work?" *Harvard Business Review*, Vol. 60, No. 1, pp. 105-114.

NASA (2000a). "NSTS 1988 News Reference Manual," http://science.ksc.nasa.gov/shuttle/technology/sts-newsref/stsref-toc.html#, Author, Kennedy Space Center, FL, accessed: 14.8.2007.

NASA (2000b). "Spaceport Systems Processing Model: Introduction to Space Shuttle Processing," Author, presented 4 February, Kennedy Space Center, FL.

NASA (2006). "2006 NASA Strategic Plan," http://www.nasa.gov/about/budget/index.html, NASA Headquarters, Washington D.C., accessed: 14.8.2007.

National Science Board (2002). *Science and Engineering Indicators – 2002*, National Science Foundation, Arlington, VA, Ch. 6, p. 6.

Nayyar, P.R. (1993). "Stock Market Reactions to related Diversification Moves by Service Firms seeking Benefits from Information Asymmetry and Economies of Scope," *Strategic Management Journal*, Vol. 14, No. 8, pp. 469-591.

Ng, J. (2007). "Airbus sees higher costs at China assembly plant," *The Wall Street Journal*, Vol. 115, No. 153, 7-9 September, p. 6.

References

Olsen, R.F. & L.M. Ellram (1997). "A portfolio approach to supplier relationships," *Industrial Marketing Management*, Vol. 26, No. 2, pp. 101-113.

Ouchi, W.G. (1981). *Theory Z: How American Business Can Meet the Japanese Challenge*, Addison-Wesley, Reading, MA.

Parmigiani, A. (2007). "Why do Firms both Make and Buy? An Investigation of Concurrent Sourcing," *Strategic Management Journal*, Vol. 28, pp. 285-311.

Pennings, J.M. (1994). "Interfirm linkages and globalization," in: Shrivastava, P., A. Huff & J. Dutton (Eds.), *Advances in strategic management*, Vol. 10, JAI Press, Greenwich, United Kingdom, pp. 329-335.

Peteraf, M.A. (1993). "The Cornerstone of Competitive Advantage: A Resource-based View," *Strategic Management Journal*, Vol. 14, pp. 179-191.

PIMS (1977). *Selected Findings from the PIMS Program*, Strategic Planning Institute, Cambridge, MA.

Phillips, D. (2005). "Airbus and Boeing: Dueling visions," *International Herald Tribune*, 12 January, http://www.iht.com/articles/2005/01/11/business/AIRBUS.php, accessed: 10.8.2008.

Płaczek, E. & J. Szołtysek (2006). "Outsourcing as a Form of Partnership Relations," *Electronic Scientific Journal of Logistics*, Vol. 3, No. 4, http://www.logforum.net, accessed: 20.1.2008.

Polak, C. & S. Belmondo (2006). "Japan R&D Policies and Programs in the Aeronautic and Space Sectors," SERIC, Tokyo.

Prahalad, C. & G. Hamel (1990). "The Core Competence of the Corporation," *Harvard Business Review*, Issue May-June, pp. 79-91.

Pritchard, D. (2001). "The global decentralization of commercial aircraft production: implications for US-based manufacturing activity," *International Journal of Aerospace Management*, Vol. 1, pp. 213-226.

Quinn, J.B., T.L. Doorley & P.C. Paquette (1990). "Technology in services: Rethinking strategic focus," *Sloan Management Review*, Vol. 31, No. 2, pp. 79-87.

Quinn, J.B. & F.G. Hilmer (1995). "Strategic outsourcing," *The McKinsey Quarterly*, Vol. 1, reprinted from the Sloan Management Review, pp. 48-70.

Rappaport, A. (1986). *Creating Shareholder Value*, Free Press, New York.

Razvi, N. (2007). "Business Process Expert – Business KPIs," SAP, https://wiki.sdn. sap.com/wiki/x/x4Y, Walldorf, Germany, accessed: 2.2.2008.

Rebitzer, J.B. & L.J. Taylor (1991). "A Model of Dual Labor Markets When Product Demand is Uncertain," *The Quarterly Journal of Economics*, Vol. 106, No. 4, pp. 1373-1383.

Richardson, J. (1993). "Parallel sourcing and supplier performance in the Japanese automobile industry," *Strategic Management Journal*, Vol. 14, No. 5, pp. 339-350.

Rothaermel, F.T., M.A. Hitt & L.A. Jobe (2006). "Balancing Vertical Integration and Strategic Outsourcing: Effects on Product Portfolio, Product Success, and Firm Performance," *Strategic Management Journal*, Vol. 27, pp. 1033-1056.

Rowan, V. (2004). "How Joint Ventures Are Organized, Operated on International Construction Projects," presented at Overseas Construction Association of Japan (OCAJI), 29 July, London.

Rumelt, R.P. (1982). "Diversification strategy and profitability," *Strategic Management Journal*, Vol. 3, No. 3, pp. 359-369.

References 113

Saltelli, A., S. Tarantola, F. Campolongo & M. Ratto (2004). *Sensitivity Analysis in Practice: A Guide to Assessing Scientific Models*, John Wiley & Sons, Chichester, United Kingdom.

Schmidt, K.M. (1996). "The Costs and Benefits of Privatization: An Incomplete Contracts Approach," *Journal of Law, Economics, & Organization*, Vol. 12, pp. 1-24.

Scholes, M., M. Wolfson, M. Erickson, E. Maydew & T. Shevlin (2005). *Taxes and Business Strategy: A Planning Approach*, Third Edition, Prentice Hall, Englewood Cliffs, NJ, Ch. 11-12.

Schumpeter, J.A. (1989). *Essays: On Entrepreneurs, Innovations, Business Cycles, and the Evolution of Capitalism*, Transaction Publishers, New Brunswick, NJ.

Shepherd, W.G. (1972). "The elements of market structure," *Review of Economics and Statistics*, Vol. 54, pp. 25-37.

Sherry, L. & L. Sarsfield (2002). "Redirecting R&D in the Commercial Aircraft Supply Chain," Issue Paper, RAND, Santa Monica, CA.

Shinde, S. (2007). "Deutsche Firmen agieren sorglos: Wirtschaftskriminalität: Studie beziffert Schaden auf jährlich sechs Millionen Euro – Gefahr in Schwellenländern am grössten," *Handelsblatt*, No. 199, 16 October, p. 19.

Slansky, D. (2005). "Outsourcing Changes the Face of Industry," *Automation World Magazine*, Chicago, p. 60.

Slay, A.D., H. Alberts, R.F. Bescher, W. Gibbs & W.L. Harris (1999). *Defense Manufacturing in 2010 and Beyond: Meeting the Changing Needs of National Defense*, National Academy Press, Washington D.C., Ch. 3.

Smith, C. & L. Wakeman (1985). "Determinants of Corporate Leasing Policy," *Journal of Finance*, Vol. 40, No. 3, pp. 896-908.

Smith, C. & R. Watts (1982). "Incentive and Tax Effects on U.S. Executive Compensation Plans," *Australian Journal of Management*, Vol. 7, pp. 139-157.

Smith, D.J. (2001). "European retrospective: the European aerospace industry 1970-2000," *International Journal of Aerospace Management*, Vol. 1, pp. 237-251.

Smitka, M.J. (1991). "Competitive Ties: Subcontracting in the Japanese Automotive Industry," Columbia University Press, New York.

Spengler, J.J. (1950). "Vertical Integration and Antitrust Policy," *The Journal of Political Economy*, Vol. 58, No. 4, pp. 347-352.

Teece, D.J. (1992). "Competition, cooperation, and innovation: Organizational arrangements for regimes of rapid technological progress," *Journal of Economic Behavior and Organization*, Vol. 18, pp. 1-25.

The White House (2000). "Goals for a Partnership in Aeronautics Research and Technology," US Office of Science and Technology Policy, Washington D.C.

The White House (2006). "Fact Sheet – Statement on National Space Transportation Policy," US Office of Science and Technology Policy, http://www.ostp.gov/other/launchstfs.html, Washington D.C., accessed: 14.8.2007.

Thompson, P. (2001). "How much did the Liberty Shipbuilders learn? New evidence for an old Case Study," *Journal of Political Economy*, Vol. 109, pp. 103-137.

Tirole, J. (1988). *The Theory of Industrial Organization*, MIT Press, Cambridge, MA, pp. 15-60.

Todeva, E. & D. Knoke (2005). "Strategic alliances and models of collaboration," *Management Decision Journal*, Vol. 43, No. 1, pp. 123-148.

References   115

Trochim, W.M.K. (2006). "The Research Methods Knowledge Base: Measurement," Second Edition, http://www.socialresearchmethods.net/kb, Cornell University, New York, accessed: 16.1.2008.

Tullock, G. (1980). "Efficient rent seeking," in: Buchanan, J.M., R.D. Tollison & G. Tullock (Eds.), *Toward a theory of the rent-seeking society*, Texas A&M University Press, College Station, TX, pp. 97-112.

US Congress (1995). *The Lower Tiers of the Space Transportation Industrial Base*, OTA-BP-ISS-161, Office of Technology Assessment, Government Printing Office, Washington D.C.

US Department of Commerce (1995). *1992 Census of Manufactures Industry Series - Aerospace Equipment, Including Parts*, Bureau of the Census, Economics and Statistics Administration, Author, Washington D.C., p. 17.

US Environmental Protection Agency (1998). "Profile of the Aerospace Industry," EPA/310-R-98-001, Author, Washington D.C.

Van Aken, E.M. & G.D. Coleman (2002). "Building Better Measurement," *Industrial Management*, Vol. 44, No. 4, pp. 28-33.

Venkatesan, R. (1992). "Strategic sourcing: to make or not to make," *Harvard Business Review*, pp. 98-108.

Weigel, A.L. & D.E. Hastings (2004). "Measuring the Value of Designing for Uncertain Future Downward Budget Instabilities," *Journal of Spacecraft and Rockets*, Vol. 41, pp. 111-119.

Wernerfelt, B. (1984). "A Resource-based View of the Firm," *Strategic Management Journal*, Vol. 5, pp. 171-180.

Wessner, C. (Ed.) (1999). *Trends and Challenges in Aerospace Offsets*, National Research Council, National Academy Press, Washington D.C.

White, S. (2000). "Competition, Capabilities, and the Make, Buy, or Ally Decisions of Chinese State-Owned Firms," *Academy of Management Journal*, Vol. 43, No. 3, pp. 324-341.

Wilhelm, S. (2001). "Local aerospace suppliers applaud Boeing strategy," *Puget Sound Business Journal*, 30 March.

Williamson, O.E. (1967). "Hierarchical Control and Optimum Firm Size," *Journal of Political Economy*, Vol. 75, No. 2, pp. 123-138.

Williamson, O.E. (1975). *Markets and Hierarchies: Analysis and Antitrust Implications*, Free Press, New York.

Williamson, O.E. (1985). *The Economic Institutions of Capitalism*, Free Press, New York.

Woo, C.Y. & G. Willard (1983). "Performance representation in business policy research: discussion and recommendation," presented at the 23rd Annual Meetings of the Academy of Management, Dallas, TX.

Wright, T.P. (1936). "Factors Affecting the Cost of Airplanes," *Journal of the Aeronautical Sciences*, Vol. 3, No. 4, pp. 122-128.

Yan, A. & M. Zeng (1999). "International joint venture instability: a critique of previous research, a reconceptualization, and directions for future reseach," *Journal of International Business Studies*, Vol. 30, pp. 397-414.

About the Author

Dr. Dr. Robert A. Goehlich was born in Berlin, Germany, in 1975. He studied Aerospace Engineering at the Technical University Berlin from 1996 to 2000 and received his doctoral degree in Engineering in 2003. He has done research stays and consulting in the fields of jet engines, reusable launch vehicles and space tourism at the Israel Institute of Technology (Haifa, Israel), at the University of Washington (Seattle, USA), at the National Aerospace Laboratory (Tokyo, Japan) and at EADS Space (Kourou Spaceport, French Guiana). Robert A. Goehlich created and lectured the world's first "Space Tourism" Master's and Ph.D. courses as a visiting professor at Keio University (Yokohama, Japan) from 2003 to 2005. He was also involved in JAXA's Future Space Transportation System Team concerning cost optimization and in NASA's "Moon, Mars and beyond" vision concerning "Economic Development of Space" project. Since 2006 he has led various projects at a leading aerospace company. In 2008, he received his doctoral degree in Economics at the European Business School (Oestrich-Winkel, Germany).